Greenhill Books

UNIFORMS
OF THE
GERMAN SOLDIER

UNIFORMS
OF THE
GERMAN SOLDIER

AN ILLUSTRATED HISTORY

FROM 1870 TO THE END

OF WORLD WAR I

Alejandro M. de Quesada

Greenhill Books, London
MBI Publishing, St Paul

Greenhill Books

Uniforms of the German Soldier
An Illustrated History from 1870 to the end of World War I

First published in 2006 by Greenhill Books/Lionel Leventhal Ltd,
Park House, 1 Russell Gardens, London NW11 9NN
and
MBI Publishing Co., Galtier Plaza, Suite 200,
380 Jackson Street, St Paul, MN 55101-3885, USA

British Library Cataloguing-in Publication Data available

ISBN-10 1-85367-708-6
ISBN-13 978-1-85367-708-3

Library of Congress Cataloging-in Publication Data available

For more information on our books, please visit www.greenhillbooks.com,
email sales@greenhillbooks.com, or telephone us within the UK on 020 8458 6314.
You can also write to us at the above London address.

Typeset by Ian Hughes

Printed and bound in China by Compass Press

CONTENTS

COLOR ILLUSTRATIONS

INTRODUCTION

The Kaiser's Army, 1870–1919

Germany's military history has captivated historians for generations. She went from being a strong military power to a vanquished nation only to rise again, like the phoenix, and become strong once more. The study of the uniforms of the German soldier during these periods of glory, defeat, and rebirth shows a gradual change, despite a steady trickle of influence from the past that permeates these decades.

While much has been written on the uniforms of the Kaiser's Army during World War I and on Hitler's Wehrmacht during World War II, virtually nothing has been done on German uniforms during the era of peace from 1871 to 1914, the Colonial and overseas troops, the Reichswehr, the Nationalen Volksarmee, and the Bundeswehr. Furthermore, in recent years no attempt has been made to show the continuation of uniform styles from the earliest days of the German Empire to the present, showing the steady changes of uniform and covering periods that are not familiar to the general public. The closest attempt was made over seventy years ago by Richard and Herbert Knötel and Herbert Sieg's *Handbuch der Uniformkunde*, published in 1937. While this book has become the main primer for anyone wanting to study military uniforms, its coverage stops prior to World War II.

The aim of this book is not to challenge this classic reference work but to complement it. The general history of the German Army and its uniforms presented here uses contemporary photography rather than drawings, showing the uniforms and equipment as they really appeared. In addition, by including a general history and a description of the uniforms it is possible to understand the latter in their context and examine the reasons why particular styles were retained, replaced, or reworked during periods in the existence of the German Army. It was impossible to include every single type of uniform, insignia, headgear, and equipment used in the last 130 or so years; however, this work attempts to illustrate styles and traditions that have been handed down from the earliest days to today's German Army. Hopefully this book will be a useful reference to the novice as well as the advanced military historian.

Prussia's Emergence as a Military Power

In the decades following the decline of the Holy Roman Empire, the Kingdom of Prussia emerged as the dominant player in Central European politics. Prussia had first been settled and Germanized during the thirteenth and fourteenth centuries by the Teutonic Knights, a military Order of German monks that overran the Slavs in the region. The Knights were eventually defeated by the Poles and Lithuanians at the battle of Tannenberg in 1410; however, in the course of the next century the Hohenzollern dynasty that ruled Brandenburg (with Berlin its seat of power) came to dominate Pomerania, Silesia, West Prussia, and eventually much of the Rhineland and Westphalia.

Germany's military heritage was carefully created by a succession of Prussian rulers in the seventeenth and eighteenth centuries. The first of these was the great Elector, Frederick Wilhelm (1640–88), who recognized that a standing army with a professional officer corps was the key to the development of a powerful state in his remote part of the Empire. His grandson, Frederick Wilhelm I (1713–40), doubled the size of his professional army to ninety thousand and added a trained reserve of conscripted peasants, forming one of the most modern and efficient fighting armies in eighteenth-century Europe. The Army was supported through heavy taxation, which consumed 80 per cent of peacetime state revenues. Frederick II (1740–86), known to posterity as Friedrich der Große (Frederick the Great) or "Alte Fritz", raised the strength of the Prussian Army to 150,000 and fought a series of wars between 1740 and 1763. By wresting control of the province of Silesia from Habsburg Austria, Prussia had become one of the most powerful continental states and a rival to the Habsburgs for domination over the myriad of German kingdoms and provinces.

The officer corps and its aristocratic character were established early in the eighteenth century as Prussian kings tried to gain the support of aristocrats, known as *Junkers*, by permitting them virtual control over the selection of officers. A cadet school was established in Berlin in 1733 to train sons of *Junkers* to be officers. Eventually the officer corps was on its way to becoming the most privileged social class in Prussia.

The militarism of Prussia inspired a multitude of feelings – respect, fear and hatred – among other European states and peoples. Under the strong leadership of a self-perpetuating and career-oriented general staff, the Prussian Army rarely had to endure any interference in its affairs by the civil government. However, the Army's failure to reform and lack of preparedness after the death of Frederick II in 1786 led to its decisive defeat by Napoleon Bonaparte's forces at Jena in October 1806.

General Gerhard von Scharnhorst oversaw the revitalization of the Army in the years following Jena. Reforms included ending dependence on mercenaries and introducing compulsory military service. The officer corps was expanded to include commoners, and officers were encouraged to take greater initiative in battle. The new Prussian Army distinguished itself at the battle of Leipzig in 1813 and again at Waterloo in 1815, where, under the command of Field Marshal Gebhard von Blücher, the Army was instrumental in Napoleon's final defeat.

Prussia's reputation for military efficiency was re-established by the Army's final victories over Napoleon. The Prussian War College (Kriegsakademie) became a model for military staff colleges around the world in the early nineteenth century. A book of that era, *On War* by the Prussian general Karl von Clausewitz, became a classic, its theories of land warfare still studied by officers of many armies more than 160 years after its author's death.

Prussian-led victories over Denmark in 1864, Austria in 1866 and France in 1870–1 were followed by the unification of the various German states into the German Empire (1871–1918). Seeking recognition of equal status from Great Britain, France, Russia and Spain – the states that comprised "old Europe" – the new German Reich was characterized by a rising surge of patriotism, as can be seen in the creation of organizations such as the Pan-German League, the Colonial League and the Navy League. Powerful industrialists such as Krupp began to wield considerable influence with the German imperial government. Otto von Bismarck became imperial Germany's first chancellor and began to mastermind a series of aggressive policies. Following the formation of imperial Germany, the legendary Prussian General Staff became the German General Staff. This body was a center of great power in the highly militaristic regimes of Kaiser Wilhelm I (1858–88) and Kaiser Wilhelm II (1888–1918), ignoring Clausewitz's dictum that civilians should control the military. Within the first years of Kaiser Wilhelm II's reign the parliament (Reichstag) had lost all direct control over the military, and by 1914 even the Ministry of War had been reduced to an essentially administrative role. By the outbreak of war in August 1914, the German Army was one of the largest in the world, with well over 662,000 soldiers on active duty, and an additional fifteen thousand reservists and thirty thousand officers. The forces of Prussia, Bavaria, Saxony and Württemberg combined amounted to over twenty-four army corps. Their high standard of training, the widely held belief that other nations were preventing Germany from assuming its role as a world power, and the militarization of German society, toughened the population for a war. Germany was like a coiled spring.

Uniforms of the Kaiserheer, 1871–1918

Describing the uniforms worn by imperial German soldiers from 1871 to 1914 is a complicated business, since there were many variations across the different regiments and German kingdoms. Basically, Hessian, Prussian and Saxon infantrymen wore dark-blue, single-breasted tunics, while those from Württemberg were the same colour but double-breasted. The tunic sported scarlet piping on the skirts at the rear and down the front; on Saxon tunics it was round the bottom of the skirts. As a special distinction, Prussian Guard Regiments wore two bars of white lace (*Kapellenlitzen*) on their scarlet-colored collars. A number of other regiments, including those from Bavaria and Saxony, wore these bars in white or yellow lace. Sleeves might have Swedish or Brandenburg-style cuffs, the colors differing according to regiment. Brandenburg cuffs were normally worn by the infantry, while Swedish cuffs tended to be worn by the artillery, cavalry, and pioneers. There were, however, numerous differences and exceptions to the norm from kingdom to kingdom. For example, a Bavarian infantryman wore a light-blue tunic, whereas his Saxon equivalent, say a member of the 108th Saxon Regiment, wore a dark-green tunic. With the notable exception of Bavarian infantrymen, who wore light-blue trousers, most German infantry units wore dark-grey, almost black, trousers with scarlet piping down the legs. Infantry battalion and company distinctions were identified by the color of the cloth knot affixed to the bayonet frog.

Field artillerymen wore a uniform similar to that of the infantry. The coat was dark blue with black collars and cuffs with red piping. The shoulder-straps were scarlet, while the trousers were dark grey. Saxon artillerymen wore dark-green tunics with a scarlet collar, cuffs and piping. The foot artillery wore the same uniform as the field artillery, with the sole exception that their shoulder-straps were white. Saxon foot artillery wore scarlet shoulder-straps.

German cavalry uniforms were as varied as those worn by the infantry. There were three basic types of cavalry: Heavy (Cuirassiers), Medium (Lancers/Uhlans) and Light (Dragoons, Hussars and Light Horse). Each Cavalry Regiment wore a distinctive regimental uniform. The Cuirassier Regiments took their name from the cuirass they wore. The Guard Regiments' cuirasses were copper-colored, while those of other regiments were of black iron. Cuirassiers wore a white tunic with regimental stripe facings on the collar, down the tunic front and on the Swedish cuffs. The Guard Regiments wore the usual *Kapellenlitzen* of white lace on each side of the collar and miniature versions of the double bars on the cuff. Their pantaloons were made of white kersey and their overalls of dark-grey cloth with scarlet piping. When mounted, the men wore leather thigh-boots. Imperial German Dragoons wore a similar tunic to that of the Prussian infantry, with the difference that it was light blue in color. The tunic's front, skirts, shoulder-straps and Swedish cuffs were piped with the regimental colors. Their pantaloons were dark blue and their overalls dark grey with scarlet piping.

The Hussars wore a tunic, its color varying from regiment to regiment; it was cut short, with five rows of lace or braided cord on the chest. The collar and cuffs were the same color as the tunic, with trimming and, in the case of the Guard Hussars, yellow lace. The uniquely shaped buttons found on the lace or braided cord were of metal or wood. Only the 3rd, 15th, and Guard Hussars Regiments were entitled to the dolman-pelisse that was worn loosely over the left shoulder suspended by lace or chain. Their pantaloons were dark blue. A low busby of sealskin with a colored bag was worn by all Hussars, and white hanging plumes were worn as part of the full dress uniform. Most Uhlans or Lancers wore a dark-blue, double-breasted tunic with piping of the color of the facings and pointed Polish cuffs with a button near the point. However, the Bavarian Uhlans' tunics were dark green and those of Saxony were light blue. A pair of metal epaulettes with a cloth center and backing were a distinctive feature of the uniform. Regimental colors were featured on the tunic's collar, cuffs and turnback, and under the surface of the epaulette. As a regimental distinction, the 17th and 18th Lancers wore metal shoulder-scales.

At the outbreak of World War I airship personnel wore the uniform of the Prussian Guard Pioneer Battalion, with a shako and Guard *litzen* on the collar and cuffs. The Flying Troops, who were founded during the Great War, wore a large variety of uniforms, since many of the officers and men had been pulled from other sectors of the Army. However, standardization of uniforms was begun in the latter part of the war. Officers wore winged propeller insignia on their braided shoulder-boards with a light-grey underlay, while enlisted men wore a winged propeller over their unit number (Bavarian flying units had only the insignia without the unit number) embroidered or chain-stitched into their cloth shoulder-straps. Piping colors on the shoulder-boards designated the battalion – white for the 1st Battalion, red for the 2nd Battalion, yellow for the 3rd Battalion and blue for the 4th Battalion. In addition, some flying units wore their numerical designation in the form of an oval patch on the left sleeve of the tunic and greatcoat. The designation consisted of the group number in Roman numerals over the squadron number in arabic numerals for bomber units, and "F" over arabic numerals for flying detachments. Field airship detachments consisted of a script "L" over the depot battalion number. Anti-aircraft platoons consisted of a winged artillery shell or "MG" (for *Maschinengewehr* or Machine Gun) for Prussian units, and for Bavarian units "FLK" and "MG" in red chain-stitch on their shoulder-straps. While Bavarian flying units wore a plain collar, all personnel in Prussian and other flying units wore the *Kapellenlitzen* of Guard Regiments. Seconded officers wore the winged propeller insignia on the shoulder-boards of the original regimental uniforms of their previous service. Hence in some unit photographs we are treated to the interesting spectacle of a variety of officer uniforms – for example, *Litewka*, *Überrock*, *Attila*, and other field-grey uniforms – all in one sitting. Early in the war, a variety of cold-weather clothing was used by pilots and their crews, many donning civilian fur coats and motorcycle crash helmets. In 1917 field-grey flight coveralls were authorized.

Military chaplains and field rabbis were designated as senior military officials without rank distinctions. On 3 June 1913 a field uniform was authorized for them. It comprised a knee-length field-grey frock coat with stand-up collar, barrel cuffs and violet piping on the collar, tunic front and cuffs. A Red Cross armband – white-edged violet for Christian chaplains and white for Jewish rabbis – was worn on the left sleeve of the frock coat. Military chaplains and rabbis wore a colonial-style Model 1907 Wide-Brimmed Felt Hat with violet brim edging and band as well as the Model 1910 Officer's Peaked Cap with violet band and crown piping. For Christian military chaplains both hat and cap had a white enamelled cross between the state and national cockades, while Jewish rabbis wore no distinctive insignia. Military chaplains and field rabbis also carried visible symbols – the Protestant cross (silver), the Catholic crucifix (black with silver edging) and the Jewish Star of David suspended from a silver chain. In 1915 the eight buttons of the frock coat were changed from matt grey to matt white.

By the middle of the nineteenth century, royal ladies began to make official appearances in versions of military uniforms. The idea of noble ladies as honorary chiefs of regiments originated in Germany, where this distinction was conferred on royal personages and distinguished generals and statesmen. These ladies often donned the uniform of their corps and rode at the head of their regiments. Queen Victoria was the honorary chief of the 1st Dragoons of the Prussian Guard, but she never wore the light-blue tunic of the regiment. However, several princesses of her family held positions as chiefs of German regiments and wore their uniforms. The German Empress Frederick, a daughter of Queen Victoria, sported the uniform of German regiments, as did her successor, the last German Empress and wife of Kaiser Wilhelm, who was chief of the Schleswig-Holstein Fusiliers and also of a Circassian Regiment; looking particularly attractive "in the pretty white tunic of the latter, and with a three-cornered hat, her Majesty was often seen on parade". Queen Margharita of Italy, Crown Princess Sophia of Greece and Princess Frederick of Hesse followed suit, as did Russian royal ladies – both the Dowager Empress and the Empress, a granddaughter of Queen Victoria. Crown Princess Marie of Romania, daughter of the Duke of Saxe-Coburg-Gotha (better known as the Duke of Edinburgh), was honorary colonel of the 4th Romanian Hussars, and wore their uniform. Queen Alexandra and the Duchess of Connaught both held honorary colonelcies of German regiments, but the Queen did not wear the uniforms concerned.

The ladies' regimental uniform usually consisted of the correct male-style tunic with high neck and epaulettes, but with left-hand buttoning, and a woman's skirt, riding-style in the case of mounted regiments. Headgear varied from feminine versions of military caps to the *Pickelhauben*, complete with spike and, for the Tsarina, resplendent plume. In addition, noble ladies were permitted to wear medals, decorations and orders on their regimental uniforms, thereby completing their militaristic appearance.

Officers' rank distinctions were found on their shoulder-boards with pips. Gefreite wore a small button on each side of the collar. Unteroffizier or non-commissioned officers wore lace around the bottom of the collar and cuffs. Feldwebel or Cavalry Wachtmeister wore a pair of large buttons over the Unteroffizier lace on the collar. Vizefeldwebel wore the same distinctions as the Feldwebel but with an additional band of lace above each cuff. The Offizierstellvertreter wore in addition to the Vizefeldwebel distinctions a metallic braid around their shoulder-straps with metal unit designations. A Fähnrich had Unteroffizier distinctions but with an officer's sword knot (portepee).

On 23 October 1842 Prussia adopted the leather helmet with a metal spike ornament known as the *Pickelhaube* for its armed forces, and soon afterwards for its fire and police organizations as well, which were run on military lines. The different German states began to adopt the helmet, beginning with Oldenburg (1843), and then Hansestädte (1845), Sachsen-Altenburg (1845), Sachsen-Weimar-Eisenachm (1845), Reuss (1845), Anhalt (1846), Sachsen-Meiningen (1846), Hessen-Kassel (1846), Mecklenburg-Schwerin (1848), Mecklenburg-Strelitz (1848), Schleswig-Holstein (1848), Hannover (1849), Nassau (1849), Baden (1849), Hessen-Darmstadt (1849), Sachsen (1867), Württemberg (1871), and Bayern (1886). This style of helmet was also adopted by some civil organizations in nearby Austria-Hungary.

The *Pickelhaube* replaced the bell-crowned shako that had been worn by all Prussian infantry and Guard units. The first model, the M1842 Helmet, was constructed of heavy leather with reinforced side panels. The front visor was squared and the rear visor covered the neck. It was tall, typically measuring about thirty-seven centimeters. A tall brass spike was affixed to a cruciform base on the crown of the helmet (the base was then secured by stud retainers, star-shaped for officers and round for enlisted men). A raised neckband (*perlring*) was secured around the narrow base of the spike proper. A leather rosette or cockade in the colors of the German state was affixed to the right side by the knurled bolt that also served as support for the scaled chinstraps.

The Prussian *Pickelhaube* was modified in 1856. The chinscales were flattened (although convex ones were still used by cavalry, administrative personnel and regimental officers). The knurled bolts were replaced with a new retainer for securing the chinscales to the body of the helmet, while the cockade was reduced and began to appear in metal. The helmet's ungainly height was reduced in 1857 and again in 1860.

After field experience in the campaigns against Denmark (1864) and the Austro-Hungarian Empire (1866), the design of the *Pickelhaube* underwent several further changes. In 1867 the squared front visor was replaced by a rounded visor for the infantry regiments. The base plate of the helmet, once cruciform in design, was now rounded. The Prussian cockade was reduced in size. The metallic spine was also removed from the helmet. Only Dragoon officers and generals continued to wear the squared visor.

After the Franco-Prussian War, the failure of helmets to retain their shape was addressed in a directive of 23 November 1871 which called for the replacement of the rear spine. It was to be secured by a rivet in the rear visor and a screw post in the crown of the helmet. The scaled chinstraps of enlisted men's helmets were to be secured by threaded and notched screws, while those of officers were to be mounted by push-through posts. It was not until 1887 that a new model of *Pickelhaube* with many significant changes was issued for enlisted personnel.

The *Pickelhaube* worn by imperial German field and foot artillery regiments differed from that worn by the infantry only in that the spike was replaced by a ball. In full dress, the Guard Artillery wore white horsehair plumes, the horse and Saxon Artillery black plumes and the Bavarian Artillery scarlet plumes.

Cuirassiers wore a special *Pickelhaube* of yellow metal or white steel that descended very low behind the head and curved backwards to cover the nape of the neck, with a square front peak and a metal-scale chinchain. All Cuirassier Regiments wore the spike, but for the two Guard Regiments in full dress the spike was replaced with a white metal crowned eagle.

Dragoons wore a similar *Pickelhaube* to the infantry, except that the front peak was cut square with metal binding and the chinscales were of metal. The Uhlans, however, wore a type of *Pickelhaube* known as a *tschapka* or *czapka*. This helmet had a lacquered leather body with a tall, raised, four-cornered mortarboard top. The cloth facings matched the epaulette uniform facings. The visor trim of the helmet was of brass or German silver matching the color of the plate. Officers' *czapkas* were trimmed with silver or gold piping on the mortarboard. Cords were worn, secured to a leather knot on the top of the helmet. The scale chinstraps were mounted by screw retainers or the Model 1891 Posts. The *Reichskokarde* was worn on the right post of the *czapka* and the *Landeskokarde* was worn on the mortarboard. In 1915 the chinscales were replaced with black leather straps, and the fittings were issued in a pewter-colored field-grey finish. A variety of Uhlan *czapkas*, from metal to felt, were made during World War I, until all such decorative forms of headgear were phased out of service in 1917.

Many German states in the years preceding and following World War I used the standard Model 1881/91 leather helmet shell; the ornaments made the headgear distinct from state to state. Each helmet had the *helmwappen* (helmet plate) of a province or a distinctive regimental plate. On some *Pickelhauben* a *Landeskokarde* showing the province's color was attached to the sides of the shell. The *Pickelhaube* was virtually obsolete by the time World War I broke out.

An interesting earlier type of headgear was the crested helmet known as a *Raupenhelm*, adopted around 1803 by Bavaria during the Napoleonic Wars. The black leather helmet was similar to an earlier model that had been adopted in 1789. The helmet had a small plate on the front with a crown above, and a small chinchain, fastened on each side by lion's-head bosses. The plate was later replaced with the royal cipher in 1848. By the time of the Franco-Prussian War Bavarian troops wore a modified crested helmet with a leather chinstrap, binding around the peak, and a crowned "L" cipher. The helmet was replaced with the *Pickelhaube* in 1886.

Another type of headgear that was considered to be distinctively German was the shako or *tschako*. The shako had been the standard form of headdress for the Jäger and Schützen units since the Napoleonic Wars. In an *Allerhöchste Kabinetts-Ordre* (AKO) of the Prussian Army in 1854 a new pattern of shako was introduced. Enlisted personnel wore a shako made of black leather, while officers wore one with a fine black cloth cover. A field badge or cockade, black and white in color (for Prussia), was worn on the peak of the headgear, and a helmet plate affixed to the front. At the time there were only three styles of plates worn with the shako. Jäger Battalions 1, 2, 5 and 6 wore a ciphered "FWR" device, while Guard units wore a German silver Guard star. Other Jäger units wore a device with a brass button securing a vertical bar of braiding or *litzen*. The shako was designed to take brass or (for officers) gilded chinstraps. A parade plume of black and red was authorized for Sunday and parade service. The plumes were secured behind the cockade and fanned out, dangling forward slightly to add a drooping effect.

In 1860 a new shako was introduced for use in the Prussian Army. The front and rear visors were reduced in size, a black leather chinstrap was authorized for enlisted personnel, and rosettes were added. A new brass shako plate for Jäger Battalions 1, 2, 5 and 6 was adopted, consisting of a heraldic Prussian eagle with the "FWR" cipher in a shield on the eagle's breast. A simple "FR" cipher on the eagle plate was to be used by the other Jäger units. In addition, a bandeau inscribed "MIT GOTT FÜR KOENIG UND VATERLAND" (With God for King and Country) was authorized and incorporated into the Jäger plate. Further additions to the shako were also made: ventilation holes were added in 1888, infantry-style chinstraps in 1892, post mountings for the enlisted *Pickelhaube*-style chinstraps in 1895, and the black, white and red *Reichskokarde*, to be worn on the right post of the shako, was authorized in 1897. While on field maneuvres, special cloth field covers that were cut specially to permit the wearing of the field badge were worn over the black leather shakos. In April 1915, during World War I, the fittings were switched to pewter trim.

The origins of the visorless field cap (*feldmütze*), resembling a "pillbox" and worn by enlisted personnel, date from the Napoleonic Wars. Before World War I the color of these caps was the same as the tunic, and they were piped with the color of the appropriate branch of service or regiment. By 1910 all field caps were field-grey in color, with a red band and piping on the crown for infantry and a black band with red piping for artillery, pioneer, and other specialist units. Commissioned and non-commissioned officers wore the same field caps as enlisted personnel, although theirs had a visor. By 1915 the officer's peaked cap had a grey-green visor and chinstrap. The Model 1917 Officer's Standard Peaked Field Cap was adopted for all branches of the Army, and consisted of a dark greenish-grey band and crown piping, while a field-grey band and piping were used by Bavarian troops. All styles were worn with state and national cockades. In addition, special unit insignia were worn with the enlisted and officer caps. Ski troops of the Alpenkorps wore an Austrian Army metal edelweiss flower on the left side of the green cap band, while military administration officials wore a Hohenzollern eagle between the state and national cockades, members of the Carpathian Corps wore a scroll between their cockades inscribed "KARPA-THENKORPS", with binding paired antlers and pine branches, and members of the 8th Bavarian Reserve Division wore a blue-and-white Bavarian shield on two silver holly leaves on the left side of the cap. Additionally, the 17th Brunswick Hussar Regiment and the 1st Life Hussar Regiment wore their distinctive regimental badges on the field-grey undress caps.

In essence, the German Army had a standard uniform by the time World War I began in August 1914. The introduction of field-grey uniforms for all German troops began as an experiment in 1907, and selected units were issued with the trial uniforms. The new uniforms were successful, and the German General Staff made them the official service dress of the German Army in orders of 23 February and 18 March 1910. The cut of the tunic was basically the same for artillery, infantry and train. The color of the early tunics was much lighter and less green than that which became typical during the war. The Jäger and Schützen Regiments received grey-green uniforms. The buttons and metal fittings, such as belt hooks, on the Model 1910 Tunic were made of dull brass or silvered metal. The tunics had their own distinctive piping or *Waffenfarben* – red for infantry, pioneer and machine-gun units; green for Jäger and Schützen (although the Prussian Guard Machine-Gun Unit was permitted to retain black piping for collar and cuffs); scarlet for artillery; and light blue for train. The uniform collar, *litzen* and so on were basically the same as the peacetime uniform. General officers had their traditional gold embroidery on red collar patches, while non-regimental (staff) officers wore plain collar patches in the color of their peacetime tunic collar. Field tunics continued to use the three cuff styles, Brandenburg, Swedish and Saxon. Company or squadron numbers were placed on the buttons of the shoulder-straps, while the tunic buttons bore crowns or heraldic emblems. Each of the cavalry branches (Uhlans, Hussars and Cuirassiers) retained their own distinctive characteristics in the newly adopted field-grey uniforms.

In 1915 a simplified version of the Model 1910 Uniform was first issued. The cut remained basically the same, as did the collar and shoulder-straps, but the distinctive cuffs were replaced by plain-back or barreled styles, and the piping on the rear skirt was discontinued. On 21 September 1915 a new, simplified field uniform was introduced. In addition, field-grey greatcoats without collar patches were issued, as were stone-grey trousers (field-grey for Bavarian troops). The new Model 1915 Field Blouse consisted of a fly front that concealed its buttons; rank distinctions were still restricted to the collar and, occasionally, the shoulder-straps. It was in essence the old *Litewka* Model 1893 of Boxer Rebellion vintage, slightly modified from dark blue to field-grey, and was issued in large quantities to Landsturm units at the outbreak of World War I. The same order also abolished the colorful distinctive regimental uniforms. A considerable number of full-dress uniforms in field-grey were made and stored away in order to be donned after the war, only to be worn later on by some officers and members of the Freikorps during Germany's post-War revolutionary period. The Model 1915 Field Blouse was modified with the addition of breast pockets, and used by ski companies as well.

The Model 1916 Steel Helmet or *Stahlhelm* was widely distributed, and soon replaced all other forms of protective headgear used by the imperial German forces during the war. This helmet and its variants would become the new symbol of Germany and its military from 1916 onwards. Covers for the M-16 Pattern Helmets were of grey or white cloth and had a reinforced leather ventilation hole through which the helmet "horn" fitted. In addition, the helmet was often painted with an angular camouflage pattern. In 1918 a "special" steel helmet was introduced with cutouts along the leading edge of the distinctive pattern helmet. The cutouts were designed to offer protection to telephone talkers in the trenches, allowing them to wear the bulky helmet while also holding headsets to their ears. In the Weimar era, this style of helmet seems to have been issued from old stock to Reichswehr cavalry and artillery units. A plain leather chinstrap was utilized in the 1916 and 1918 Pattern Steel Helmets.

After 1916 the *Pickelhaube* was no longer issued, and surplus quantities were later modified and issued to German fire-fighting units or *feuerwehr*. The shako was later adopted by the Prussian and other German state police forces after the war, and remained in service well through the Weimar and Nazi eras. After World War II both

East and West Germany continued to use the shako, until it was finally phased out in the 1970s. The shako, then, was one of the most versatile and enduring forms of headgear in German service.

Germany as a Colonial Power

Germany possessed four colonies in Africa – German East Africa (Tanzania), Togoland (Togo), Kameruun (Cameroon), and German Southwest Africa (Namibia). In addition, Germany maintained colonial interests in the Pacific region – New Guinea, Samoa, and Tsingtao (China). All were lost to Great Britain, France, the United States and Japan in the course of World War I. All four African colonies were the scenes of conflict between the natives that dwelled there and the German colonial troops, called *Schutztruppen*.

The *Schutztruppe* was one of the smallest colonial forces in the world, even smaller than the forces of Portugal and Belgium. In 1900 it numbered only three thousand officers and men, and in 1914 it had 6,461 officers and men, of which fourteen companies were stationed in East Africa, nine companies in Southwest Africa and twelve companies in Cameroon. Togoland, however, had a paramilitary police organization rather than a *Schutztruppe*. In times of need the *Schutztruppe* would receive aid from German Marines (*Seebataillon*) stationed abroad, from German warships patrolling in the area or from regular Army units sent to the colonies from Germany itself.

The officers and NCOs of the *Schutztruppe* were white, regular officers and NCOs from the German Imperial Army. There were considerable incentives to serve with the *Schutztruppe*. The pay was good, and it was a chance to see exotic lands and military action, which appealed to bored officers in peacetime Germany. The enlisted men, or *askaris*, were local natives. They generally enlisted for an initial five-year term and then re-enlisted on a yearly basis. The *askaris'* uniform was khaki, and they were armed with either the Mark 71 or 84 Model Single-Shot Rifle. They were very loyal and well trained. The Germans stressed discipline and marksmanship. In the field, the *askaris* were taught to fight as a company.

In 1884, German trading companies founded all four German colonies in Africa. Within several years they proved unable to cope with the problems of running a colony, so the Imperial German Government took over their administration. The Germans' desire to push inland and expand their holdings led to conflicts with the natives and the creation of the *Schutztruppe*. For the next twenty-odd years, there was almost always fighting in at least one of the colonies. The numerous and varied skirmishes, campaigns and wars with the native tribes are reminiscent of the American Indian Wars. Small groups of German troops patrolled and attempted to control a vast amount of land. As the colonial wars were numerous, only the more major conflicts will be described here.

Three principal campaigns were fought by the *Schutztruppe* in East Africa: the Abushiri Rebellion in 1888–90, the Hehe War in 1891–8 and the Maji-Maji Revolt in 1905–7. German involvement in Cameroon began in 1884, when trade treaties were signed with Dovala chiefs along the coast. Conflicts with tribes living in the interior ensued, and the Germans created a *Poliztruppe* in November 1891 to combat the hostile natives. The Dohomey troops mutinied against the new acting governor, Leist, a brutal man who had treated them badly and, when they had complained about poor pay and terrible food, ordered their wives to be publicly whipped. The government in Germany founded the *Schutztruppe* in Cameroon on 9 June 1895. Togoland's paramilitary police force was very similar to the *Schutztruppe*: the soldiers wore khaki dress, were armed with Model 71 Mauser Rifles, and their officers were regular German Army men who referred to them as soldiers, not policemen. The police force was divided into platoons based on the tribal background of the men. In 1914, it consisted of two officers, six NCOs and 560 enlisted men.

Events in Cameroon were typical – the fighting consisted of small wars against rebellious or independent-minded tribes. The most ardent opponents of the Germans were the Dagombe, who resented German control over traditional trade routes. In 1877, they rebelled against the Germans along with their allies, the Konkomba, who were aggrieved at the loss of tribal lands. In May, Lt Valentine von Massow and a force of ninety-one police marched into the area to quell the revolt. They were attacked at Adibo by between six and seven thousand Dagombe and Konkomba warriors. Again, it was the combined use of machine-gun and small-arms fire and discipline which saved the day for the Germans. Some five hundred natives were killed, and their forces scattered. Shortly after the battle of Adibo, Massow and his men took the Dagombe capital, Yenbli, and burned it. The rebellion soon ended.

Some of the heaviest fighting witnessed by German colonial troops was to take place in German Southwest Africa. Made a protectorate in 1884, because of its extensive plains and grazing lands Southwest Africa was viewed as an area for German settlement. The German *Schutztruppe* almost immediately began to move inland in order to secure lands for German farmers and settlers. Also in the colony were large numbers of natives, divided into several large tribal groupings. In the north were the Ovambi, in the central region were the Herero, and in the south were the Mama, or Hottentots. All of the tribes were semi-nomadic cattle raisers. The first real opposition to the Germans came from one of the Mama subdivided tribes, the Witbooi, led by Hendrik Witbooi. Hendrik refused to sign a treaty of peace and opposed further German encroachment into their lands. German officials in the colony called upon the *Schutztruppe* to force Hendrik Witbooi and his people to sign.

The *Schutztruppe* in German Southwest Africa had been created in 1890, and was commanded by Captain Curt von Francois. Eventually it would consist of nine field companies, one of which was mounted on camels, and three light batteries of artillery. However, at the start of the Witbooi conflict Captain Francois had few men, and required reinforcements from Germany before the campaign could begin. Reinforced, Captain Francois planned a surprise attack upon Hendrik Witbooi's stronghold at Hornkranz. On 12 April, Captain Francois's force arrived outside Hendrik's fortified city. Francois split his command, ordering the first company to attack the city from the east and the second company to attack from the north. After the defense, which lasted approximately three hours, Hendrik ordered the city to be abandoned. Behind them they left 150 Witbooi dead. The German forces returned to Windhoek in triumph, but their victory was short-lived. In retaliation, the Witboois attacked a German horse post and drove off or captured most of the German horses. For the time being the German forces were left on foot, and the well-mounted Witboois were now hard to catch. Even after a further hundred men arrived from Germany in June 1893, Captain Francois seemed unable to regain control over the situation. In August, the Witboois ambushed a supply train of twenty wagons and destroyed it completely. In the following six months after the battle of Hornkranz, Hendrik was stronger than ever, with six hundred men, four hundred rifles and three hundred horses at his disposal.

In August, the newly promoted Major Francois now felt he could move against the Witboois. He planned to surround the Witboois, isolate them, then draw them into a confrontation and defeat them. However, the mobile Witboois kept slipping away while skirmishing with the Germans and raiding their rear areas. Losing confidence in Major Francois, the German government decided to replace him with Major Theodor Leutwein. Leutwein arrived in German Southwest Africa in February 1894. He did not immediately move against the Witboois, instead spending time meeting with, negotiating with and winning over neighboring tribes. He began to regain German control over the region while at the same time severing aid and support to Hendrik. In May Leutwein persuaded Hendrik to agree to a truce which was to last until the end of July. Leutwein hoped he could negotiate the Witboois into surrender; if not, the break would nevertheless allow time for additional German reinforcements to arrive. The Witboois did not capitulate, and the final confrontation was now at hand. Hendrik and his followers had retreated to the Naukloof Mountains and fortified their positions there. Leutwein blocked off the various mountain passes, thereby stopping any possible escape, and advanced into the Naukloof Mountains. The battle of Naukloof started on 27 August and became wide-ranging, roaming over rough terrain. The control of waterholes and advance points on the high grounds were contested by both sides. Unable to retreat and having lost the last of the Witboois-controlled waterholes, Hendrik surrendered on 9 September 1894. The Witboois conflict had proven to be an unpleasant experience to the Germans, but nothing like the next campaign, which would rock the colony.

A number of factors had led to unrest amongst the Herero: there had been an epidemic in 1897 which had killed half of the Herero cattle herds, and German settlements were putting mounting pressure on various tribes to move. On 12 January 1904, the Herero, led by Chief Samuel Maherero, revolted at Okahandja. The *Schutztruppen* under Leutwein were taken completely by surprise by the revolt. Leutwein's forces consisted of forty officers and 726 soldiers divided into four companies of mounted infantry and one artillery company. He also had a reserve of thirty-four officers and 730 enlisted men, four hundred German settlers with no military training and 250 native scouts and auxiliaries. His troops were armed with the Gewehr 1888 Rifle, and in addition there were five quick-fire, five older artillery pieces and five Maxim machine guns. There were also a number of small walled forts consisting of an armory, barracks and watchtower. Major Leutwein and three companies were in the extreme southern part of the colony, over four hundred miles away, subduing a small revolt by the Bondelzwort, when the Herero struck. With little opposition from the overstretched German colonial authorities, the rebellion in the north spread rapidly, destroying isolated farms and ranches and attacking most of the German settlements and forts in the region. Okahandja and Windhoek were briefly placed under siege. Between 19 January and 4 February, German troops were able to relieve both cities, but were not strong enough to take the offensive. Reinforcements arrived, consisting of Marines from the cruiser *Habicht* on 18 January. Sufficiently reinforced for Major Leutwein to put 2,500 men in the field, the Germans began a three-column counter-offensive in April. The columns were named the eastern, western and main. However, the newly arrived German troops were not conditioned for the climate, and soon proved to be ineffectual against the seasoned Herero. With so little success, Leutwein finally called off the offensive to await more reinforcements; in the meantime, the German government removed him and ordered General Lothar von Trotha, a seasoned colonial officer who had fought in East Africa and China, to take command of the colonial forces.

Von Trotha arrived on 11 June. During the months of May and June, large reinforcements arrived until von Trotha had approximately ten thousand men and thirty-two pieces of artillery. General von Trotha was able to accomplish what Leutwein had been unable to do: encircle the Herero with a large force. The Herero began to dig defenses at the Waterburg Mountains and prepare for their final battle.

The battle commenced on 11 August, when the Germans advanced into the mountains. The artillery bombarded the Herero positions, causing heavy losses. The infantry converged on several fronts, thus making it hard for the Herero to fight everyone at once. Unable to resist any longer, the Herero finally broke out and retreated into the desert, therefore ending the rebellion.

Just as one uprising ended another had begun. The Mama revolted in October under Hendrik Witbooi, now eighty years old. The Mama numbered 1,000–1,500 men, with only one-third armed with rifles. German troops now numbered seventeen thousand. Despite the imbalance of numbers, a long and arduous guerrilla campaign was waged, with over two hundred skirmishes and engagements. During the course of the revolt, Hendrik Witbooi was killed near Tses, and leadership passed to Jacob Morenga. The revolt was eventually put down, and the fighting ended in 1907. With this final campaign, the German colonial wars in Africa ended. In fact, the Germans would control their colonies for only another ten years, until World War I ended their colonial empire.

Uniforms of the Imperial German Colonial and Overseas Troops

In German East Africa from 1889 to 1891, troops raised under the authority of the Reichskommissar wore white tropical helmets with the national cockade of black, white and red. The basic uniform was white for service and a dark-blue tunic with turndown collar and brass buttons for full dress. The full dress tunic also had twisted shoulder-cords of silver, black, and red, as well as between one and three gold rank stripes on the cuffs, with the top row in the form of a loop. Officers wore sashes and sword knots embroidered in silver, red and black. In addition, a khaki service dress of the same pattern was worn, and NCOs' ranks were denoted on the left upper arm with one to three chevrons. The *askaris* wore a red fez with a blue tassel or turban, single-breasted khaki tunics and blue puttees. All leather equipment of the *askaris* and *Schutztruppen* in the German colonies was brown. Following the incorporation of the colonial troops of German East Africa into imperial service, the following uniform was adopted from 1891 until 1896.

For full dress, the officers wore a *Pickelhaube* bearing an imperial German eagle plate and chinscale in yellow metal, and a dark-blue single-breasted tunic with gold buttons, white piping on the turndown collar, tunic front, Brandenburg cuffs and skirt-pocket flaps, and a gilt imperial crown at the end of each collar. The sash and shoulder-straps were similar to those worn by the *Seebataillon*. Dark-blue trousers with white piping were worn. The fatigue or daily uniform was a white tunic with dark-blue piping and breast and skirt pockets. Tropical helmets were white, and worn with a brass spike and imperial German eagle plate. In addition, a white cap with a dark-blue band and a national cockade was worn by all ranks. In the same style as the white uniform, a khaki service dress with yellow piping and imperial crowns at the ends of the collar were used by the troops when in the field. British-style chevrons were used to denote NCO ranks. The uniform of the *askaris* remained unchanged.

From 1889 to 1893, the troops of the Reichskommissar in German Southwest Africa wore jackets and trousers of grey cord. Between 1893 and 1896, when this force entered imperial service, a light-blue collar and pointed cuffs were added to this uniform, with a white loop of Guard lace (officers wore silver) on a red patch. Up to 1895 a small, French-style kepi made popular in the American Civil War was worn, with a blue band and piping around the top and a black rectangular leather visor; the German national cockade of black, white and red was affixed to the front.

In 1896 a general pattern uniform was introduced for the *Schutztruppen* and became standard for most of the troops stationed in the various German overseas colonies. The home service uniform was a tunic of light-grey cord with stand-and-fall collar, Swedish cuffs and piping in the color of the colony (white for German East Africa, light blue for German Southwest Africa and red for Cameroon). In addition, light-grey trousers with the colony's piping was worn with the tunic. A broad-brimmed grey hat with a band bearing the color of the colony became the symbol of the German colonial soldier. The hat was turned up at the right side, with a large black, white and red metal cockade fastened to the flap. On the collar and cuffs of the tunic white Guard lace (silver for officers) with a red patch was worn. The sword knot, shoulder-straps and sash were in the national colors, in styles similar to those used by the Kaiser's army in Germany. Officers wore a double silver aiguillette on the left shoulder of their full dress uniform. General officers had traditional Prussian-style red distinctions with gold embroidery, gilt buttons and gold hat binding.

The service dress of the German colonial troops consisted of a khaki jacket with a row of white metal buttons bearing the imperial "squared" crown, turndown collar and round cuffs – piped with the appropriate colony's colors, with no lace – khaki trousers and a khaki tropical helmet bearing a cockade on the front. The *askaris* wore a similar uniform, with dark-blue or khaki puttees. A khaki fez with a neck flap was adopted, with a silver or brass German imperial eagle plate affixed to the front. As the distinctive color of the *Schutztruppen* in Cameroon was red, it was found on their uniform's piping, rank chevrons, and the bandsmen's wings worn by the native troops. The police troops in Togo wore the same uniform. All leather equipment and footwear were brown.

In 1850 a *Marinirkorps* was raised in the Prussian Navy, and in 1854 it was renamed the *Seebataillon*. It was composed of infantry and artillery carried on board ship. From 1867, the German Imperial Marines were strictly an infantry unit. The *Seebataillon* survived the transition from confederation to imperial troops in 1871. The numbering of the units began with the 1st in 1883, followed by the 2nd in 1889 and the 3rd in 1898. The *Seebataillonen* began to see service in the German African and overseas colonies – the 3rd Sea Battalion was called in as part of the Allied Relief Expedition during the Boxer Rebellion of 1900, and after that was stationed in the German colony of Tsingtao, China. On 29 August 1914, the 1st and 2nd Sea Battalions, home-based in Wilhelmshaven, were assigned to a special Naval Division, which also included units of the Marine Artillery and some other naval formations. Throughout World War I the Naval Division fought in most of the battles on the Western Front, including Flanders. On 10 November 1914, the 3rd Sea Battalion surrendered to Japanese Forces after a spirited defense of Tsingtao – losing one-third of Germany's marine force in the process. With the Armistice on 11 November 1918, the *Seebataillonen* were no more. When the German armed forces were reorganized in 1919, no provision was made for Marine Infantry.

Beginning in 1850, the uniform worn by units of the *Seebataillon* consisted of a dark-blue tunic with self-colored collar and Brandenburg cuffs. The front of the coat, collar, and the three-button scalloped skirt pocket flaps were piped in white. Officers wore white-piped cuff patches and a loop of old Guard lace on the collar. On the officers' epaulettes and other ranks' white shoulder-straps was a foul anchor. The trousers were dark blue with white piping. From 1856 to 1867, there existed a special *Seeartillerieabteilung*. It wore the same uniform as the *Seebataillon*, but with black collar and cuffs. Anchors with two crossed cannon barrels above them were worn on the shoulder-straps. Until 1862, the *Seebataillonen* wore a *Pickelhaube* like that of the line artillery, with a brass plate. This was replaced with a blue-covered felt shako with a black leather peak, bearing a bronze anchor badge with the motto "MIT GOTT FÜR KOENIG UND VATERLAND". The shako plate was altered in 1875 with the addition of the imperial eagle over the anchor, and brass chinscales were added to the shako. In 1883 the shako was modified with leather front and rear peaks. Officers' shakos were of black cloth, while those of other ranks were of lacquered leather. For full dress a black plume – red for musicians – was worn on the shako. Initially, the dark-blue visored cloth caps with white piping around the top of the band were worn with the initials "KM" on the front. In 1875 white bands and piping around the top were introduced to the cap. From 1854 a cockade was worn, with the national colors of red, white and black becoming standard after 1871.

From 1875 white collars and cuffs were worn on the tunic, and in 1888 officers and men adopted two loops of Guard lace on the collar and three on the cuff patches. The Guard lace was in gold for officers and yellow for the men. An imperial crown over two crossed anchors was affixed to the men's shoulder-straps and the officers' epaulette crescent. After a while, battalion designations in Roman numerals were added below the crossed anchors. Officers wore a gold imperial crown on their shoulder-straps. From 1906 onwards the lapels for officers were faced with white. On the field-grey Model 1910 Uniform the *Seebataillon* wore white piping on the cuffs, shoulder-straps, front of the coat and collar, with yellow Guard lace on the collar and cuff patches. The shoulder-strap for enlisted men consisted of an imperial crown over crossed anchors and the battalion designation in yellow embroidery. With the adoption of the Model 1915 Field Blouse the men wore yellow Guard lace on a white collar patch. The *Seebataillon* wore the same greatcoat as the Army. Leather equipment and footwear were black. For service in China and other tropical climates, khaki uniforms were worn, with a stand-and-fall collar and shoulder-straps. In addition, a tropical helmet bearing the brass shako plate of the *Seebataillon* was worn with the uniform. A national cockade was fixed below the plate. Leather equipment and footwear were brown.

During the Boxer Rebellion, Germany provided troops for the Allied armies waging the various campaigns in China. At the start of the Rebellion in June 1900, there were sailors from the East Asian Squadron, the 3rd Sea Battalion, a Kommando detachment, and a battery of Marine Horse Artillery. The East Asia Brigade, consisting of two infantry brigades, was quickly established and sent off to China under the command of General Graf von Waldersee. In addition, there was a Field Artillery Regiment, a mounted regiment of Uhlans, and a pioneer battalion with railroad-engineer and telegraph companies. Sanitation, train, munitions, and other support troops completed the complement of the East Asia Brigade. General von Waldersee's forces arrived at Taku on 21 September 1900 and remained in China until 7 September 1901 and the official declaration of the end of hostilities. The remaining troops of the East Asia Brigade and of the 3rd Sea Battalion returned to Tsingtao.

The uniforms of the East Asia Brigade were officially field-grey, but a wide variety of materials, shades, and styles were worn by the troops. Generally, the *Litewka* or jacket was of a slightly darker shade than the trousers and the hat. The Model 1892 *Litewka* was of field-grey cloth and fastened down the front by six horn buttons. There were four large pockets on the front of the jacket and, unusually, two on the rear. To improve wear, the two lower pockets were lined with leather and were intended for carrying cartridges. For all branches the collar, front seam of the jacket, and pocket flaps were piped in poppy red. The Jägers' jacket piping was light green. Reversible shoulder-straps were used for both field and garrison duties. For garrison duty the shoulder-straps used the following colors and emblems: infantry had white with the unit's number stitched in red, Jägers light green, cavalry poppy red, artillery poppy red with a red grenade, pioneer poppy red with a red "P", and railroad troops poppy red with a red "E" and lightning bolt. When in the field, troops reversed their shoulder-straps to show the field-grey body piped in either light green for Jägers or poppy red for all other branches. In addition, the Model 1893 *Litewka* was used by some troops. The jacket was dark blue, a front flap concealing the six horn buttons, and was issued with and without four flap pockets on the front. The shoulder-straps previously mentioned were also used with this coat, although the reverse for field use was dark blue. This coat and its later variants would later influence the adoption of the Model 1915 Field Blouse during World War I. Khaki uniforms for summer service were basically the same styles used by the *Schutztruppe* and *Seebataillon*. Shoulder-strap colors remained the same for field and garrison duties when worn on the khaki uniforms.

The most common headgear worn by members of the East Asia Brigade and colonial troops was the tropical helmet or *tropenhelm*, a khaki cloth helmet with a cork body and removable ventilator. The frontplate was of imperial colonial style in brass. The *Waffenfarbe* coloration on the cap band denoted branch of service, white for infantry and black with red piping for artillery, and a national tricolored cockade was affixed to the right side of the helmet. The cloth neck flap or havelock was removable, and designed to protect the wearer's neck from the South China sun. Troops also wore a floppy straw hat with the brim turned up and pinned to the wearer's right side; it sported a large German national cockade and, immediately beneath, a small cockade of the soldier's home province.

In addition, enlisted members of the Imperial German East Asiatic Infantry wore a *Pickelhaube* consisting of a grey-green cloth cover over a leather body with grey leather-beaded front and rear visors. It had a brass-trimmed spike, base, and stud retainers, a brass colonial eagle and grey leather chinstrap with brass fittings secured to Model 1891 Posts. The frontplate was common to all imperial colonial units. A single *Reichskokarde* was worn on the helmet's right side. Contingents from the other German provinces that formed the East Asiatic Forces used this helmet, with their respective state helmet plates and cockade. The following brass plates have been observed with the East Asiatic *Pickelhaube*: Baden, 92nd Brunswick Regiment (1st and 2nd Battalions), Prussia (Regiments 74, 77, 78, 164 and 165) and Württemberg.

The Imperial German East Asiatic Jäger and other enlisted services wore a shako whose helmet body was composed of green leather with green cloth sides. The front-plate was the familiar brass colonial service eagle. A brown leather chinstrap with brass buckles was worn, secured to brass Model 1891 Posts. The field badge or cockade was in black, white and red, as befits colonial troop units. The Jägers adopted a flat-topped sun helmet for their tropical kit, apparently attempting to pattern it after their shako. The body was khaki over cork with a reinforced, stitched bead on the front visor and a flip-up rear visor. The helmet plate, in brass, was the colonial services eagle. The top of the helmet was a ventilator button, and a cockade was secured to the right-hand side of the helmet. A color band was also used.

With the outbreak of World War I in August 1914, Germany sent troops to aid her allies of the Austro-Hungarian and Turkish Empires. Regular German forces were sent to Palestine, Sinai, Bulgaria, Macedonia, and Greece. Many of the troops were issued with khaki drill uniforms, or had normal continental uniforms modified for hot climates.

Troops serving in Macedonia and Palestine wore tropical helmets in brown drill with or without the colonial-style imperial German eagle plates commonly worn by the *Schutztruppen*. In addition, a helmet band was worn with a large national cockade affixed to the front or side, similar to those worn during the Boxer Rebellion – many might have been surplus items from that conflict. The color of the helmet band was white for infantry and black with red piping for artillery. Later, General der Kavallerie Otto Liman von Sanders, commanding the German troops in Palestine, issued orders for the tropical helmet to be replaced by a brown drill cap, to avoid confusion with British troops who wore similar headgear. These caps were worn with or without removable havelocks and were fashioned with brown leather chinstraps and visors. The cap bands were black with red piping for artillery, plain drill for infantry, and blue with red piping for train troops. The caps were designated as the Model 1916 Tropical Cap with regular peak and the Model 1918 Tropical Cap with the larger peak.

The uniform was varied but consisted mainly of a lightweight khaki drill jacket. The brown drill jackets had turned-down collars, breast and hip pockets, and six metal buttons down the front. Another version was similar in construction but had only two hip pockets and no breast pockets. A notable feature of these tunics was the clear stitching of field-grey thread on the hip pockets and the front of the coat. This becomes even more distinctive when the tunic has faded, almost to a yellowish color, under the blazing desert sun of the Middle East. Today many military historians and collectors apply the term Model 1916 Tropical Tunic to the above-mentioned pieces in order to differentiate those used by the Colonial, Marine, Naval, and East Asia Expeditionary Forces. The following shoulder-straps were used with the khaki tunic: artillery had scarlet piping and red grenades or numerals; infantry had either piping in army corps colors with red numerals or plain khaki; medical troops had dark-blue piping; train had blue piping. Trousers were of the same material as the jackets and were worn with puttees and brown ankle boots. Surplus colonial uniforms and equipment were also utilized by these troops.

Troops serving on the Macedonian and Serbian Fronts wore a felt ersatz spiked helmet. It was an all-pressed-felt construction with pressed-felt visors. A field-grey "pewter" metal regimental unit plate was secured to the front of the helmet, bearing the designation "R 22" (22nd Infantry Regiment). It had field-grey Model 1891 Posts with a matching spike base and ventilation top, and a black leather chinstrap with grey metal lugs and buckles. In addition troops wore another modified *Pickelhaube* variant made of cork and with a white cloth covering. The fittings were of wartime "pewter", and consisted of a spike base with a lug mount showing and a grey metallic frontplate with a regimental designation only. A brown leather chinstrap was worn, secured by alated side-split brad retainers. The havelocks made for these helmets are particularly interesting.

As the German states were united and collectively became a colonial power in Africa and the Pacific, the German soldier became the symbol of the nation's prestige and honor. Many nations around the world, especially in Latin America, admired the professionalism of the Teutonic militaristic bearing of the Imperial German Army. Military missions from Germany were sent all over the world to train foreign armies, many of which adopted the military uniforms, equipment and even the military traditions of the German Army. To this day one can still see Chilean or Ecuadorean soldiers dressed in Imperial Prussian-style uniforms and *Pickelhauben*, as well as bandsmen carrying "Jingling Johnnies" and goose-stepping down the main boulevards during national events. Throughout the twentieth century the Mauser bolt-action rifle was the weapon of choice for most nations of the world, and was only replaced by the Russian AK-47/AKM-style assault rifles in the latter part of the century. The golden era of German influence on other countries' uniforms, equipment and weapons began with Germany's victory in the Franco-Prussian War and ended with the Armistice and the abdication of Kaiser Wilhelm II. Civil war and social upheaval followed, after which Germany's fledgling democracy emerged. The military itself underwent changes, reinventing itself several times, and appeared to be in search of its soul – looking for a clear purpose to its existence in a world its monarch had now departed. In less than two decades the German Army would find its long-awaited Messiah – Adolf Hitler.

ALEJANDRO M. DE QUESADA

COLOR ILLUSTRATIONS

Above. A Prussian soldier from one of the Guard Regiments with a Model 1860 *Pickelhaube*, photographed in 1866

Above right. A soldier from the 1st Bavarian Infantry Regiment wearing the Prussian-style uniform adopted in 1872. Note the *Raupenhelm* or "Caterpillar" helmet on the left

Right. A soldier from Hessen wearing the Prussian-blue uniform with Swedish-style cuffs prescribed for artillery and pioneers. Note the cockade colors of white and red for Hessen. He is wearing a crowned belt-buckle and black belt

Above. Prussian artillerymen posing with their fieldpiece. Note the ball on top of their *Pickelhauben*

METZ. - La Compagnie des Drapeaux
Abmarschieren der Fahnenkompagnie nach Frescaty

No 497 - Edité par G. Forissier, Metz

Far left. Prussian infantrymen wearing the blue tunics that were adopted by most of the German Confederation after 1872. Note the straight French-style cuffs, often referred to as Brandenburg-style, even though they have a more "scalloped" appearance. They are wearing musicians' wings on their shoulders

Left. Bavaria adopted the *Pickelhaube* in 1886, although it differed slightly from those used by the other states. One distinctive feature was the squared front visor, similar to the type used by the Dragoons. This soldier is with the 2nd Bavarian Infantry Regiment

Above. Prussian musicians leading a detachment of standard bearers carrying their regimental standards. Note the use of gorgets by the standard bearers

Right. A soldier serving with the Prussian 7th Infantry Line Regiment

Above left. A guardsman from the 1st Prussian Guard Dragoon Regiment. He has yellow Guard lace on his collar and the crowned cipher "VIR" in yellow on his red shoulder-straps

Above. This soldier is from the 1st Guards Field Artillery Regiment, and is wearing parade dress. Note the Swedish-style cuffs with the Guards' double *Kapellenlitzen* on his cuffs, as well as on his tunic and greatcoat collars

Left. A soldier from one of the Guard Regiments

Above. Without braid around the collar, the color discs indicate that this soldier is a corporal. He is armed with the Model 1898a Bayonet. A bayonet is affixed with a bayonet knot, or portepee, bearing the distinctive colors of one of the companies of his regiment

Above right. A trooper of the Gardes du Corps in court gala dress. The ceremonial duties of the Gardes du Corps were restricted to specially selected officers, NCOs and troopers of the Leib-Kompanie and the Trumpet Corps. Special uniforms were required for these duties. The sailor is from the SMS *Vineta*, and is wearing the naval parade uniform commonly referred to as a "monkey suit" by the sailors

Right. A lance-corporal of the 3rd Hussar Regiment, as distinguished by the regimental colors of the soldier's cap and *Attila*

Kaiser Friedrich III wearing the uniform and cuirass of the one of the Guard Cuirassier Regiments. Amongst the awards, decorations and orders is the Pour le Mérite, commonly referred to as the "Blue Max", one of Prussia's and later imperial Germany's most coveted decorations

Left. Kaiser Friedrich III wearing the double-breasted *Leibrock* tunic prescribed for senior officers with the shoulder-boards for Field Marshal. He is wearing the Grand Cross to the Iron Cross and the Iron Cross First Class

Right. Major Leutwein of the *Schutztruppe* wearing the early French-style, Chasseur-style Kepi

Below. Soldiers serving in the colonial forces (*Kaiserliche Schutztruppen*) in Africa wore distinctive upturned-brimmed campaign hats and brown uniforms usually made of corduroy

Opposite above left. A major of the *Schutztruppe* wearing the Colonial Service Field Uniform. The blue band on his cap signifies German Southwest Africa

Opposite above right. A soldier from the East Asia Brigade wearing the upturned-brimmed straw hat and light-weight field jacket

Opposite below. Training new native recruits for an *askari* unit in German Southwest Africa

Above. *Askaris* serving in German East Africa. All are wearing the brown Colonial Service and Field Uniforms. Note the fez with havelock. They are armed with the obsolete Infantry Rifle Model 1871/84

Below. *Askari* field musicians in German East Africa wearing distinctive musician's wings on their shoulders. The Red Cross badge worn by the drummer on the right is that of the *Sanitätsunterpersonal* or enlisted medical personnel

Opposite above. *Askaris* of the *Schutztruppe* in German Cameroon wearing the distinctive red fez with the imperial German eagle plate on the front. Note the red chevrons of the seated *Unteroffizier* or sergeant

Opposite below. Chinese soldiers serving in the German colonial forces in China being supervised by a member of the East Asian Regiment. Note the mixture of native dress with German equipment

Right. Members of a Saxon Jäger unit wearing their distinctive shakos. Note the equipment being carried by these soldiers

Below. A Bavarian machine-gun company posing with their Maxim MG-08 Machine Guns on sled mounts

Above. Maxim Machine Guns with shields being used in the trenches. During World War I the *Pickelhaube* would be replaced by the steel helmet

Below. A fallen Dragoon trooper being assisted by a comrade. The Dragoon Tunic was cornflower blue for all except for the Hessian (23rd and 24th) Regiments. He is armed with a lance and a Model 1889 Cavalry Saber bearing the state emblem of Prussia on the hilt

Right. An artilleryman wearing his distinctive *Pickelhaube*. Note the black facing with red piping on the collar and cuffs of his service tunic

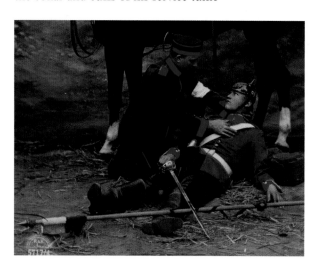

Above. A soldier's life. These infantrymen are wearing fatigue uniforms while doing their laundry and polishing their marching boots. The headgear being worn is sometimes referred to as a *Krätzchen* Field Cap

Below. A supply battalion's field bakery at work. A light-blue band and piping were worn on the field caps of the officers and men

FEEDING THE MEN IN THE TRENCHES—A GERMAN FIELD BAKERY
PHOTO © UNDERWOOD & UNDERWOOD, N.Y.

Above. A patriotic image showing a soldier wearing the Model 1910 Field Tunic with Saxon-style cuffs and bearing a flag. His oversized standard-bearer's gorget may be a photographer's prop

Above. An excellent view of the field cap worn by this enlisted man with his Model 1910 Field Uniform. The national cockade of black, white and red was placed over the state cockade, which bore its own colors

Below. Crown Prince Wilhelm inspecting captured French soldiers. Note the variety of uniforms being worn by the German officers and men

Above. A Military Policeman or Feldgendarm wearing the dark-green Model 1889 Police Tunic with Swedish-style cuffs. He has guard *litzen* and gold NCO collar-and-cuff edging braid. The infantryman on the right is wearing the Model 1910 Field Tunic with Brandenburg-style cuffs and is armed with a Gewehr 1898 Rifle

Below. French Dragoons with captured German Uhlans and Dragoons. Note the difference in uniforms

Above left. A soldier from a Landsturm Battalion guarding a pair of captured French Zouaves. Note that the soldier is wearing the dark-blue Model 1893 *Litewka* and is armed with a Gewehr 1888 Rifle

Above. Gefreiter Adolf Hitler, seated on the far right, served with the 16th Bavarian Reserve Infantry Regiment. Most are wearing the modified Model 1910 Tunics usually referred to as Model 1910/15 Tunics (Simplified)

Left. German officers in field uniforms serving in the Balkans

1

THE
GERMAN EMPIRE
(1871–1914)

Above left. A Prussian soldier of the 35th Brandenburg Fusilier Regiment in 1863. In the campaigns of 1864, 1866 and 1870–1, it had become usual to wear the trousers inside the boots while on service. The soldier is armed with a Dreyse Needle Rifle, Model 1862, and is carrying a Prussian Model 1860 Fusilier Bayonet

Above. A sapper of the 3rd Infantry Regiment Number 102 from Saxony in 1863. Wearing a similar uniform to that worn by Saxon artillerymen, his buttons are in silver instead of gold. He has his regimental number on the pompom situated on the top of his oilcloth-covered shako. Note the red, crossed pick-axes on his sleeve and the distinctive apron

Left. Kaiser Wilhelm I at the time of the Franco-Prussian War. He is seen wearing the Model 1860 *Pickelhaube* with regimental guard plate. The uniform is an officer's double-breasted frock coat, which was generally the same for all arms, being of the same color as the tunic, with a plain collar and piping on the cuffs and sometimes on the skirts as well

Above left. A Prussian infantryman in full campaign rig, *c.*1870. He is wearing the Model 1868 Line Infantry *Pickelhaube* with rounded visor

Above. A Prussian infantry NCO in 1870. His NCO lace can be seen around the collar and Brandenburg-style cuffs. To his side is his sword, which all NCOs were entitled to wear. Amongst his many decorations is a ribbon bar – the coveted ribbon of the Iron Cross Second Class, which is placed first as his highest decoration. Clearly visible is the belt-buckle or *koppelschloss* that is designated as the Model 1847

Left. A Bavarian field medic with oilcloth-covered cap in 1870. He is armed with a brass-hilted artillery short sword or *Artillerie-Faschinenmesser*. Note the Red Cross emblem on his overcoat's shoulder-straps and armband

Above. A member of an Oldenburg Infantry Regiment in 1866. His blue tunic has red-piped pointed cuffs with a button at the point. Russian-style soft caps with red piping were adopted in 1864. He is armed with an early-model Dreyse Rifle with the Model 1839 Socket Bayonet. To his side he is carrying an infantry short sword designated as the *Infanterie-Faschinenmesser* Model 1840. After 1867, Oldenburg troops wore Prussian line-infantry uniforms with light-blue piping around the cuff patches and white shoulder-boards with a red crowned "P"

Above right. A Posen Landwehr NCO in 1870. He is carrying his *Pickelhaube* with royal cipher plate. Note the distinctive early screw posts on both sides of the helmet used to secure the chinstraps. Partially visible is the brass hilt of his Model 1817/69 Infantry Sword, which was heavily influenced by the Napoleonic War-era French Model 1803 Infantry Sword

Right. A member of a Mecklenburg-Schwerin Regiment in 1870. He is wearing a Prussian-style tunic with the distinctive *Kapellenlitzen* and is carrying the Model 1817/69 Infantry Sword. Note the white horsehair plume on his Model 1860 *Pickelhaube*

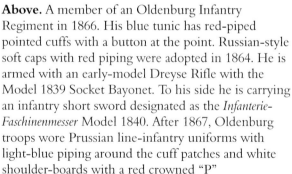

Above left. Tintype image of a Prussian infantryman armed with a Gewehr 1888 Rifle. He is holding his canteen. We can also see the back of another soldier who did not get out of the way when the photograph was taken. We can clearly see his mess-kit, Model 1887 Knapsack and Model 1871 Bayonet. Initially made for the *Infanterie-Gewehr* Model 1871 Rifle, it was reissued with the Model 1888 Commission Rifle

Above. A soldier from a Prussian Guard Regiment in 1870. Black horsehair plumes on his *Pickelhaube* were used for special occasions and parades

Left. A Prussian artilleryman with a Model 1874 Artillery Saber. Note the Swedish cuffs, black with red piping, on his tunic. The horsehair plume for the *Pickelhaube* is typical of those reserved for Line Horse Artillery Regiments

Above. This Prussian artilleryman has the Model 1860 *Pickelhaube* with the distinctive ball spike, *c.*1866. Of interest are the Brandenburg cuffs on his tunic designating him as part of the Foot Artillery (*Fuss-Artillerie*). Partially visible on his left hip is the brass hilt of his artillery short sword (*Artillerie-Faschinenmesser*)

Above right. The Prince of Hesse in the uniform of the Guard Fusilier Regiment (known as the 2nd Guard Regiment after 1830). He is wearing the Prussian-type uniform adopted in 1872, a dark-blue tunic with red piping. The pointed cuffs, also piped in red, were of basic color. On each side of the collar were two white lace loops with buttons. The buttons were in white metal. Note the distinctive rampant lion plate on the Prussian-pattern *Pickelhaube*

Right. A classic image of a Bavarian soldier with his "Caterpillar" helmet or *Raupenhelm*. The red padded wings replaced the shoulder-straps in 1860. The uniform represented here remained regulation until 1872, when Bavaria adopted the Prussian-style tunic. The distinctive helmet was replaced by the *Pickelhaube* in 1886

Above left. A priest who probably served as a military chaplain for the German Army during the Franco-Prussian War. Clearly visible is the Iron Cross Second Class with the distinctive ribbon for non-combatant recipients

Above. A Prussian Hussar, with the distinctive tunic of that service, in 1870. He is armed with the Model 1867 Cavalry Saber

Left. This officer is wearing the Prussian-style double-breasted tunic which was adopted in 1856 and remained in service, with slight changes, until 1900. The barrel cuffs were piped in red. Rank was displayed with a series of star pips on the crescent-shaped epaulettes. The upper portions of the epaulettes have a lace edging. During the short reign of Kaiser Frederick III (1883) epaulettes were not worn

Above. The Gewehr 1871 Rifle was adopted by Prussia on 14 February 1872 and became the standard rifle for troops of the German Empire. As these rifles became obsolescent, many were issued to the native troops of the imperial German colonial forces (*Schutztruppe*) and saw extensive service during World War I. This weapon accepted the Model 1865/71 (*Pionier-Faschinenmesser*) and 1871 Bayonets

Above right. The Gewehr 1871/84 Rifle was basically the same as the Model 1871 Rifle, with the addition of an eight-round tubular magazine. The rifle was short-lived and eventually replaced by the Commission Model 1888 Rifle. This rifle accepted the Model 1871/84 Bayonet, whose blade was much shorter and would become the basic design for future German bayonets

Right. A member of the 10th Field Artillery Regiment from Oldenburg, *c*.1867. The service tunic is the same as for infantry, except that the shoulder-straps and piping are red. Note the distinctive pointed cuffs with the button at the point. The grey trousers, introduced in 1858, are piped in red. Across the soldier's lap is a Model 1817/69 Infantry Short Sword, which was used by members of the foot artillery as well

Above left. Kaiser Wilhelm I wearing the double-breasted *Leibrock* tunic that nearly reached his knees. The tunic worn by General Staff officers was dark blue with a crimson collar, cuffs, piping and background to the epaulettes. Note the Kaiser's Field Marshal's shoulder-boards

Above. Kaiser Friedrich III wearing the double-breasted *Waffenrock*. The service or field cap was worn as well as the normal infantry helmet, a white plume being added when in full dress. Note the Grand Cross to the Iron Cross and the Pour le Mérite

Left. Kaiser Friedrich III in the uniform of the Guard Cuirassier Regiment

Opposite. Various images of Paul von Hindenburg, from a cadet in Wahlstatt to a senior officer serving in the General Staff during the second half of the nineteenth century. The changes in uniform through the years and his rise through the ranks are evident

Als Kadett in Wahlstatt

So rückte er 1870 ins Feld

Als frischgebackener Leut=
nant im 3. Garde=Regiment
zu Fuß

Als Bataillonsadjutant im
3. Garde=Regiment zu Fuß

Hauptmann
im Großen
Generalstab

Above left. Professor Wilms taught chemistry in the Prussian Military Academy in Lichterfelde near Berlin. Note the distinctive lace on the collar of his tunic

Above. Paul von Hindenburg as a cadet in Berlin. He first saw action in Königgrätz in 1866

Left. General Otto von Bismarck in undress or field uniform, 1870–1

Below right. An NCO from the 25th Field Artillery Regiment wearing musician's wings or "Swallow's Nests" (*Schwalbennester*). Note the regimental ciphers embroidered on his shoulder-straps

Left. Paul von Hindenburg in the uniform of Generalmajor and as Chief of the General Staff of the 8th Armee Corps, Koblenz, 1897

Above. A Bavarian infantryman wearing the Prussian-style dark-blue service uniform that was adopted in 1872. The 1st Bavarian Army Corps had white piping around the cuff patches of the Brandenburg-style cuffs. Note the new service cap with the cockade bearing the colors of Bavaria (light blue and white). The soldier is armed with a Model 1871 Infantry Dress Bayonet

Above left. An NCO musician with a Model 1874 Artillery Saber

Above. A Prussian soldier from a Guard Regiment. He has a plumed Model 1860 *Pickelhaube*

Left. A Prussian infantryman with the Model 1868 *Pickelhaube*

Above. An infantryman from the 88th Infantry Regiment (1st Battalion Mainz; 2nd Battalion Hanau) wearing the blue tunic with red collar, piping and cuffs. The buttons were of plain gilt

Above right. An NCO attached to Telegraph Battalion 2-6, 8th Company, stationed in Metz in 1885. Note the script "T" over the "8" on his shoulder-strap

Right. An NCO from a Guard Telegraph Battalion. Note the Guard double *Kapellenlitzen* on the collar and the distinctive Telegraph Unit's emblem embroidered on his shoulder-straps

Left. In 1872 Bavaria adopted the Prussian-style uniform, but retained the distinctive *Raupenhelm*. The single crown on the shoulder-straps and Guard double *Kapellenlitzen* on the collar and cuffs identifies this soldier as serving in the Leib-Grenadier Regiment. He is armed with a Model 1871 Infantry Dress Bayonet

Right. A Lancer from a Prussian Uhlan Line Regiment. The coat worn by the Uhlans was dark blue for the Prussian and Württemberg Regiments, light blue for Saxons and green for Bavarians. Note the unique *czapka* with Prussian helmet plate being worn. The field badge or cockade on the mortar-board is white and black for Prussia

Left. A trooper from the 13th King's Uhlans Regiment from Hannover. Uhlan Regiments with light-blue facings had white-piped collars, cuffs and pockets. The trooper is holding a Model 1889 Cavalry Saber

Above. A rare view of the cuirass and protective helmet used in bayonet practice in the latter half of the nineteenth century, worn here by Bavarian soldiers. They are armed with the Gewehr 1888 Commission Rifle fixed with the Model 1871/84 Bayonet. By 1886 the distinctive Bavarian *Raupenhelm* had been replaced by a *Pickelhaube* bearing the coat of arms of the Kingdom of Bavaria

Above. A Prussian Lancer with the Model 1849 Artillery Saber that was commonly used by Uhlan and Hussar Regiments. Note the cloth belt worn with the tunic

Above right. Erbgroßherzog Adolf Friedrich von Mecklenburg in the uniform of the 1st Guard Uhlan Regiment, *c.*1900

Right. A Lancer from a Saxon Guard Uhlan Regiment, possibly the 21st Uhlan Regiment. His Model 1889 Cavalry Saber has the Saxon coat of arms on the hilt's guard

Gruß aus der Sommerfrische. Zeithain.

Left. A Saxon NCO Lancer from the 2nd Saxon Uhlan Regiment (18th Uhlan Regiment). The Lancer jacket was light blue with crimson collar cuffs and lapels – which were buttoned back for full dress – while the overalls had crimson stripes. The 2nd had loops of yellow Guard lace on the collar. The *czapka* had the Saxon star on the front and a crimson cover underneath the mortarboard. The field badge or cockade was white and green

Below. Prussian Lancers of the 3rd Guard Uhlan Regiment. They wore yellow facings and piping on their tunics and *czapkas*. The NCOs are wearing stone-grey greatcoats. The collar patches of the great-coats were in the regimental facing color and the shoulder-straps in the color of the epaulette field. The Prussian Guard Regiments had the double *Kapellenlitzen* on the collar patch, while the woven ciphers and numerals on their shoulder-straps were in yellow on red and crimson material; in all other cases they were red

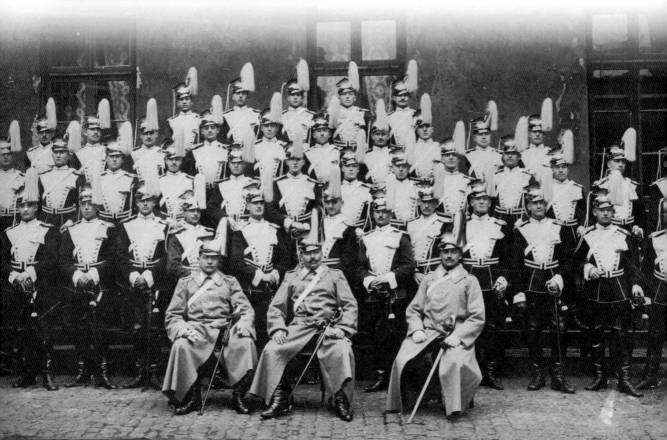

Above left. An NCO in the uniform of the 11th Uhlan Regiment. His regimental number can be seen clearly on his crescent-shaped epaulettes

Above middle. A trooper from a Bavarian Chevauleger (Light Cavalry) Regiment. These troops were dressed basically the same way as Uhlans; they wore a steel-green (*stahlgrun*) uniform but a different type of headdress – in this case, the *Pickelhaube* and not the *czapka*. Note the Bavarian Lion on the hilt guard of the trooper's Model 1889 Cavalry Saber

Above right. A Prussian corporal from a Dragoon Regiment wearing his stone-grey greatcoat over his regimental uniform. The Dragoon single-breasted tunic was cornflower-blue for all regiments except the 23rd and 24th (Hessian) Regiments. The collar, collar patches, Swedish-style cuffs and shoulder-straps were in the regimental facing colors

Right. A member of a Leib-Gendarmerie or Military Police Unit

Left above. The double *Kapellenlitzen* on his collar and the script "E" on his shoulder-strap indicate that this NCO belongs to a Guard Train Regiment

Above. An Army administration official serving in the *kriegsministerium* (War Ministry). Note the distinctive collar insignia. The uniform of the General Staff and War Ministry resembled that of the General Officers in its cut and dark-blue color. The collar, Swedish-style cuffs and all piping, however, were carmine. The collar and cuffs had two double loops of silver (General Staff) or gold (War Ministry) embroidery with bars of a leaf pattern on them. The buttons were white metal. The dark-blue trousers had triple red stripes

Left below. A Color Guard of the 17th Brunswick Hussar Regiment wearing service dress uniform. Note that he is wearing the distinctive regimental busby plate

Opposite above left. Archduke Ernst August of Brunswick in the service dress uniform of the 17th Brunswick Hussar Regiment

Opposite above right. A trooper of the 15th Hanoverian Hussar Regiment wearing gala uniform. Note the chevron on the corporal's right arm. The distinctive busby front plate of the 15th Hussars bears the battle honor "PENINSULA – WATERLOO – EL BODON – BAROSSA" on laurel leaves below the ribbon bearing the motto "MIT GOTT FÜR KOENIG UND VATERLAND"

Right. Standard bearers of a Prussian Hussar Line Regiment wearing the gala uniform with pelisses over their *Attila* (tunic). Note the use of gorgets by the troopers. All are wearing the "VATERLAND" ribbon on their busbies

Above left. A trooper from the 1st Prussian Leib-Hussar Regiment in gala uniform

Above. Crown Prince Wilhelm in the uniform of the 1st Leib-Hussar Regiment. Note the distinctive regimental skull plate on his busby and the pelisse coat hanging from his shoulders

Left. Crown Prince Wilhelm wearing the undress cap with its distinctive regimental skull insignia between the Prussian state and national cockades

Above. The Crown Prince wearing the pelisse of the Hussar Regiments

Right above. An excellent detailed study of the undress cap and pelisse. The undress cap was black with a red band and white piping

Right. A trooper from a Prussian Hussar Line Regiment. Note the distinctive black leather boots that are associated with the Hussars. The boots were ornamented at the top with white or yellow leather trim according to the button color, which formed a loop at the front. Officers wore patent-leather boots with gold or silver lace instead of braid. A rosette replaced the loop of the other ranks, who were also permitted to wear patent-leather boots for walking out

Above left. A trooper from the 9th Rhenish Hussar Regiment. Note the cockade of white and black for Prussia and the "VATERLAND" ribbon on his busby

Above. An NCO from the 9th Rhenish Hussar Regiment wearing the undress cap with regimental color and piping distinctions

Left. A trooper from the 9th Rhenish Hussar Regiment wearing the peakless undress cap

Opposite above left. This trooper is wearing the cornflower-blue *Attila* of the 9th Rhenish Hussar Regiment. The crown of his peakless undress cap was cornflower blue and the band was cornflower blue with yellow piping. He is armed with an 1879 Pattern Saber

Opposite above right. A Hussar trooper wearing the field-grey undress *Attila* that was instituted on 22 November 1909 and is usually referred to as the Model 1910 Hussar Field-Grey *Attila* Field Tunic. His sidearm is a Model 1884/98 Bayonet

Opposite below left. Crown Prince Wilhelm wearing the regimental gorget and uniform of the 2nd Queen's Cuirassier Regiment (Pomeranian). The gorget was presented to the regiment upon the 150th anniversary of the battle of Hohenfriedberg

Opposite below right. Regimental veterinarian in the uniform of the 4th Cuirassier Regiment, 1900

Above left. Colonel General Karl Einem in the white full-dress uniform of his *à la suite* commission to the 4th Cuirassier Regiment. The epaulettes of the former Minister of War bear the three stars of his rank

Above. An NCO from a Saxon Cuirassier Regiment wearing the white-plumed Pattern 1889 Enlisted-Style Cuirassier Helmet

Left. Bavarian Crown Prince Rupprecht wearing the uniform and distinctive regimental gorget of the 1st Great Elector Life Guard Cuirassier Regiment (Silesian)

Right. NCOs of the 3rd Baden Dragoon Regiment (22nd Dragoon Regiment) with an NCO of the Prussian Jäger zu Pferde Regiment. Dragoons wore cornflower-blue tunics with the regimental facing color on the collar. Dragoons wore *Pickelhauben* similar to those of the infantry, with a "squared" visor front and silver furniture on the helmet

Below right. As Germany approached the twentieth century, old and new were combined in the uniforms of the German Army. From the left, an artillery enlisted man in service uniform, as indicated by the distinctive ball on top of his *Pickelhaube* and the shoulder-strap of the 16th Field Artillery Regiment; a senior officer wearing the field-grey field uniform that was adopted in 1910; and an Uhlan wearing the distinctive *czapka*

Far right. A Prussian infantryman of the 4th Grenadier Regiment armed with the Model 1888 Commission Rifle. He is wearing the 1891 Pattern *Pickelhaube* with the visor trim in place. The chinscales confirm that this soldier is an NCO. He is wearing the dark-grey greatcoat (introduced in 1867) with collar patches and shoulder-straps

Above. Members of the 1st Guard Regiment of Foot wearing their parade-style helmets. All are armed with the Gewehr Model 1888 Commission Rifle

Far left. A Guard NCO in a stone-grey greatcoat. He is armed with the Model 1879 or Model 1883 Commission Revolver, and an officer-style sword used by NCOs

Left. soldier from one of the Guard Infantry Regiments wearing Brandenburg-style cuffs on his tunic

Above. A soldier from a Guard Jäger Regiment. In 1874 the Guard's double *Kapellenlitzen* in yellow was added to the collar and to the green Swedish-style cuffs of the tunic

Above right. An infantryman of the 115th Leib-Guard Infantry Regiment. His shoulder-strap has the initials "EL" for Ernst Ludwig. Note the distinctive belt-buckle for Hessen-Darmstadt

Right. Guardsmen of the 1st Dragoon Regiment and of a Guard Infantry Regiment. The soldier in the middle is wearing the green tunic with the Guards yellow Kapellenlitzen for a Guard Schutzen unit. The Guard Schützen units wore Brandenburg-style cuffs while the Jäger units used the Swedish-style cuffs

Above. An NCO from the 25th Dragoon Regiment in service uniform. The 17th, 18th, 23rd and 25th Dragoon Regiments had the distinction of wearing the Guard *litzen* on the collar and cuffs of their button collar. The 119th Grenadier Regiment wore a similar device on the shoulder-strap, but with different colors and facings

Above. An enlisted man from the 109th Leib-Grenadier Regiment. Note the use of the state and national cockades on the peakless field cap

Above. Men and officers from the 1st Tsar Alexander Guard Regiment marching through a Berlin street. The distinctive Miter Cap or Grenadier/Fusilier Cap for this regiment bore the Guard star under a king's crown. The 1st Foot Guards wore a similar cap

Right. A gathering of dignitaries and officers from the Guards Regiments. A senior officer of the 1st Foot Guards wearing the Miter Cap is seen conferring with a member of the Guard Infantry Regiment. The latter is wearing the Model 1910 Field-Grey Tunic

Below. Generalfeld-marschall August von Mackensen reviewing Saxon standard bearers of various regiments. Of particular interest is the Model 1890 Cavalry Guard's Helmet with a lion mounted on the top. The helmet's silver lion was awarded to the Garde-Reiter Regiment in 1907 and was to be worn when in full dress

Above left. A Bavarian Halberdier in full dress uniform with the outer vest of the Garde du Corps, serving in the royal palace of the Bavarian king, 1890s

Above. A trooper of the Prussian Garde du Corps wearing the distinctive Butcher Boots, which rose above the knee, adopted in 1856. He is wearing the red vest or *supraweste* bearing the Guard's star emblem on the front

Left. The 1889 Pattern Garde du Corps Parade Helmet had a tall, tombak Cuirassier-style body, with German silver trim on the visor. The front plate consisted of a silvered Guard star with the motto of the Black Eagle Order, "*suum cuique*" (Each to his own). The parade crowned eagle is of silver on an oval base secured with silvered plain retainer studs. Large convex tombak chinscales were secured to the helmet by Model 1894 Posts. Note that this soldier is wearing a cuirass

Above left. A Prussian soldier from the 2nd Squadron of the King's Gendarmerie wearing court dress, 1890s. The white tunic had red lapels and white lace patches with buttons

Above middle. A corporal of the Württemberg Royal Palace Company of Guards, 1890s

Above right. A Prussian corporal in the uniform of the Palace Guard Company. The uniform did not change much between 1829 and 1914

Right. A Prussian captain of the Palace Guard Company

Far right. A Prussian sergeant of the Palace Guard Company. During the nineteenth century Prussian kings had the same kind of fondness for their uniforms as they did during the era of Frederick the Great. Kaiser Wilhelm II had numerous court celebrations in the historical costumes of Frederick's day

Above. Members of a signals unit in service dress. Note the crossed signal-flag insignia on the soldier's sleeve on the far left

Below. Mounted artillerymen wearing ball-top *Pickelhauben*

Right. Artillerymen wore basically the same uniform as the infantry, but with some differences, such as the use of the Swedish-style cuffs instead of the Brandenburg-style cuffs, and the ball instead of the spike on the helmet. This soldier is wearing the white leather belt with the open-face buckle normally used by cavalry units

Below. A close-up of an artillery officer from Saxony. The white-and-green state cockade is clearly visible on the left side of his helmet. He is wearing the officer's undress uniform with his stone-grey greatcoat

Below right. A member of the Field Artillery wearing the peakless undress cap. He is holding an 1874 Pattern Artillery Saber

Right. An artilleryman from the 39th Field Artillery. Note the flaming bomb and regimental number embroidered in red on the black shoulder-straps

Below. A group of NCOs from the 75th Infantry Regiment. Of particular interest is the Prussian standard bearer with his distinctive gorget and arm-shield (*see inset*). The standard bearer's arm-shield and gorget were first introduced for use by the German Army in an *Allerhöchste Kabinetts-Ordre* (AKO) dated 15 June 1898. There were variations used by the German states and some elite units. The arm-shield ceased to exist in 1919 with the abdication of Kaiser Wilhelm II. Note the other soldiers with their shoulder-straps rolled, possibly for field maneuvers

FAHNEN & STANDARTEN DER METZER GARNISON
BEI DER PARADE AM 10. MAERZ -1813-1913- z. JAHRHUNDERTFEIER
ORIGINAL AUFN. V. FR. JOZIOR -METZ

Above. Regimental standard bearers of the Metz Garrison preparing for a ceremony, 1913. Note the use of the gorgets. The arm-shield for standard bearers is not worn on the greatcoat

Below. Soldiers of the 3rd Bavarian Infantry Regiment. Note the regimental standard bearer wearing his gorget and arm-shield (*see inset*). He would have had the Bavarian regimental standards and royal ciphers depicted on his badges of office

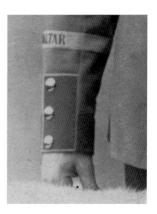

Above. A Prussian foot artilleryman armed with a Kar. 98a Rifle

Above right. A soldier from a Saxon Jäger unit wearing the unique shako and dark-green service dress. He is wearing the General Marksmanship Cord (*Allgemeine Schützenschnur*) that was introduced in 1894

Right. An enlisted man from the 73rd Fusilier Regiment Generalfeldmarschall Prinz Albrecht von Preussen (Hanoverian) wearing the "GIBRALTAR" cuff title (*see inset*). Other units entitled to wear the cuff title were the 79th Infantry Regiment von Voigts-Rhetz (3rd Hanoverian Infantry Regiment) and the 10th Hanoverian Jäger Battalion

Right. Prior to World War I, priests serving with the Army as chaplains normally wore their habits and an armband identifying their status. It was not until 1915 that a uniform for military chaplains was introduced. The chaplains wore a colonial-troop-style felt hat with the cross between the state and national cockades, and a distinctive field-grey frock coat without any rank insignia. In addition, the chaplain wore a chained cross of either a Catholic or Protestant style around his neck, and a violet armband

Below. King George V of Great Britain in the uniform of Colonel-in-Chief of the 8th Cuirassier Regiment Graf Gessler (Rhenish). Many senior officers, aristocrats and monarchs received *à la suite* commissions from elite regiments in various countries of Europe

Above. Princess Viktoria Luise of Prussia in the specially tailored uniform of Colonel-in-Chief of the 2nd Leib-Hussar Regiment. The Princess received her *à la suite* commission on 22 October 1909

Left. Kaiser Wilhelm II received many *à la suite* commissions from home and abroad. The Kaiser was a uniform enthusiast; he had many designed for himself and liked being depicted in the various uniforms in his collection. Here he is in the uniform of Field Marshal of the 1st Foot Guard Regiment. Note the specially tailored sleeve for his withered arm

Below. Kaiser Wilhelm II in the uniform of the 21st Uhlan Regiment (Kaiser Wilhelm II Koenig von Preussen 3 Saxon), for which he served as the Regimental Colonel-in-Chief. Note the Leib-Gendarme standard bearer with the Kaiser's personal standard, which was carried with him wherever he went

Above. An excellent study of the various styles of *Pickelhauben* and uniforms worn by senior officers surrounding the Kaiser

Right. A veteran Prussian Army Oberst in dress uniform. His gilt crescent-shaped epaulettes bore two rank stars and a regimental number. His decorations attest to his decades of service and campaigns, including fighting in the Franco-Prussian War

Above left. A Leutnant wearing the double-breasted Officer's Undress Uniform (*Leibrock*), 1880s

Above. Leutnant von der Linde wearing the service tunic. In time the tunic had been modified and new shoulder-boards were used. The new service tunic (*Waffenrock*) worn by this Leutnant remained in use well up to World War I

Left. A major of the 3rd Kgr. Elisabeth Garde Grenadier Regiment wearing the double-breasted *Waffenrock*. Of particular interest are the regimental insignia incorporated on the shoulder-board (*see inset*). Note the presence of the Pour le Mérite

Above left. Chief of the German General Staff Generaloberst Helmuth von Moltke's *à la suite* commission entitled him to wear this full dress uniform of the 1st Guard Grenadier Regiment

Above. A Saxon general's full dress gala uniform, worn by General der Infanterie d'Elsa

Left. Close-up of a Saxon general's full dress gala uniform, worn by General von Einem

Left. Generaloberst Alexander von Kluck in the full dress uniform of his honorary commission in the 3rd Guard Grenadier Regiment

Right. King Ludwig III of Bavaria wearing his Bavarian field marshal's Model 1910 Parade Dress Uniform with the distinctive laurel-leaf pattern in silver bullion thread on a red patch. This distinctive Bavarian collar insignia and other variations were in use until 1916, when the Prussian Alt-Larisch pattern (in silver) was adopted by Bavarian generals

2

IMPERIAL GERMAN COLONIAL AND OVERSEAS TROOPS

Above. German
Schutztruppen in various
headgear and uniforms,
*c.*1890. Clearly visible is the
imperial German crown on
the belt-buckle worn by the
reclining sergeant. Note the
use of a spike from a
Pickelhaube by the NCO in
the center

Right. Mounted troopers of
the *Schutztruppe* wearing a
variety of headgear, including
the campaign slouch hat, the
tropical busby of the Hussars,
the spiked tropical helmets
and the French-style kepis

Above left. *Schutztruppen* armed with Gewehr 1888 Rifles guarding a prisoner during the Herero uprising

Above. The Colonial Uniform Tunic in brown corduroy and the Colonial Service Uniform in brown drill. The piping of the campaign hat (as well as the band of the *feldmütze*), collar and cuffs were blue, denoting German Southwest Africa. Note the leather cartridge-belt rig for mounted troops and the mixture of the cotton drill uniform with the corduroy trousers of the standing Gefreiter

Left. A classic image of a member of the colonial troops serving in Africa. His leather cartridge-belt rig has a fixed bayonet frog. Note the bayonet knot (*Troddel*) on his left side, and a ring to attach a saber. He is armed with a Gewehr 1898 Rifle

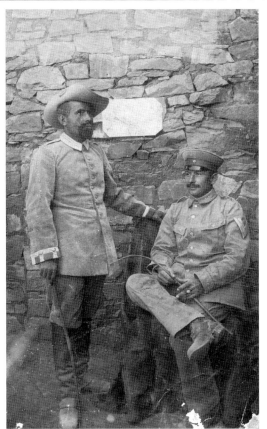

Above left. A Feldwebel with removable chevrons. Most chevrons and insignia worn on the *Schutztruppe* uniform were attached with hooks on the back so that they could be easily removed. The buttons on the service uniform were also removable

Above middle. The brim of the grey felt campaign hat was hooked to the wearer's right side and a large *Reichskokarde* was then attached to the upturned brim. The sergeant's *feldmütze* was made of corduroy with a colored wool band denoting the colony in which the soldier was stationed. A single cockade bearing the national colors was worn on the field cap's band

Above right. While stationed in Germany, members of the *Schutztruppe* would wear a stone-grey *Waffenrock* or Uniform Tunic made of wool, commonly referred to as the *Heimatuniformen* or Home Uniform. Note the colored cuffs and collar as well as the Guard's lace. The Uniform Tunic was intended for parades, walking out, and for all ceremonial occasions

Right. A close-up of an NCO wearing the *Waffenrock*. Note the silver *litzen* around the collar

Left. Another view of the stone-grey Home Uniform, worn by a veteran NCO

Below. An excellent example of various uniforms used by the *Schutztruppe* in the African colonies. Next to the white fatigue uniforms is the colonial or tropical version of the *Litewka* and the stone-grey greatcoats with Guard-style collar tabs. All are wearing *feld-mützen*

Die Welt ist weit, die Welt ist schön.
Wer weiss, ob wir uns ∞.
Wiedersehn !

4437

Above left. A close-up of the tropical *Litewka* in brown corduroy. All shoulder-straps had a "V" pattern in black red, and white with or without a wool base in the color of the colony

Above right. Members of the *Schutztruppe* in greatcoat and Colonial Uniform Tunics

Left. An Oberleutnant in the *Schutztruppe*. The only visible signs of rank are his shoulder-boards and sword

Right. An NCO of the *Schutztruppe* in the Colonial Uniform Tunic and *feldmütze* of brown corduroy. The Colonial Uniform Tunics were usually used for parades, as walking-out dress, and for ceremonial occasions while serving in the colonies

Above. Artillerymen in various types of uniform and headgear servicing a cannon

Above. A senior officer in the *Schutztruppe* wearing the Colonial Officers' Service Uniform. He is wearing the stone-grey service cap worn with the Home Uniform Tunic. The cap's band and piping were in the colors of the colony where the soldier was serving, in this case German Southwest Africa

Below. A camel rider of the *Schutztruppe* serving in German Southwest Africa in 1905. Note his leather cartridge-belt rig and holster for his Gewehr 1898 Rifle

Above left. A mounted cavalryman in full rig that was basically the same as that of the camel riders

Above right. German police and colonial officials wore similar uniforms and headgear to those of the *Schutztruppe*. Seen here is a police officer (*Landespolizei*) serving in German Southwest Africa. Note his rank, displayed on the collar and shoulder-boards. Piping for police-force field caps and uniforms in the colony was green

Below. Officers and NCOs in the German colony of Cameroon wearing their white summer uniforms. Note the standard blue piping around the collar and down the front of the tunic. In Cameroon red piping was used for headgear, in Togo yellow piping

Above. The summer uniform was worn by the *Schutztruppe* in all of its African and tropical possessions. Colonial officials adopted variations of the uniform. Note the white shoes worn by the seated enlisted man

Below. A review of native troops or *askaris* of the *Schutztruppe* serving in Cameroon. The *askaris* are wearing the distinctive red-tasseled fez with the small colonial imperial German eagle plate. They are wearing khaki uniforms with red piping on the collar and cuffs. A red bar was worn on the collar as well. Native troops in Togo, or *Polizeitruppe*, wore the same headgear and uniform but with yellow piping. Note that the officers are wearing white tropical helmets and uniforms

Above. *Askaris* serving in German East Africa and German Southwest Africa wore similar uniforms to those in Cameroon, although they wore a taller fez in khaki. The khaki fez was made with neck flaps which protected the wearer from the sun

Right. This close-up of the previous photograph shows the khaki fez with neck flap in use. The *askaris* are armed with the obsolete Mauser M1871/84 Jägerbüsche Rifle that continued to see service throughout World War I. Note the puttees worn with brown leather ankle boots

Below. *Askari* regimental band in German East Africa. Some are wearing the distinctive "Swallow's Nest" on their shoulder, identifying them as military musicians

Above. When white colonial troops received new uniforms, their old tunics were handed down to the native troops. Seen here are native troops in German Southwest Africa wearing the old Colonial Uniform Tunics minus the Guard's lace on the collar and cuffs

Below. Another view of discarded Colonial Uniform Tunics being used by *askaris* in German Southwest Africa. On closer examination, the shaded areas can be seen where the Guard's lace had been on the collar and cuffs. They are all wearing the *feldmütze* in brown corduroy. It is believed that these uniforms were used for parades and special occasions in place of the khaki uniform issued only for field use

Above. Native police troops of Kaiser-Wilhelms-Land (German New Guinea). They did not wear much of a uniform, except for a visored cap with national cockade. When they were needed in the field the colonial authorities provided limited equipment consisting of an obsolete rifle, belt with cartridge box and a mess-kit

Below. A very interesting study of uniforms worn by the *Miokesen-Schutztruppe* in Kaiser-Wilhelms-Land (German New Guinea). They are wearing naval-style jumpers with khaki visored caps bearing the *Reichskokarde*. Note the NCO on the far right wearing a rank chevron on his left sleeve

Above. Police troops in German Samoa

Below. A native police officer in one of Germany's colonial possessions in the Pacific

Right. While a part of the Navy, the men of the *Seebataillonen* or Marines wore similar uniforms to their Army counterparts. Like the *Schutztruppe*, the Marines provided additional protection to the colonies as well as Germany's interests on the seas. A few officers, such as General Lettow von Vorbeck, had the distinction of serving in the Army, the *Schutztruppe* and the *Seebataillonen*. Note the imperial German eagle with anchor and the dark-blue parade dress uniform of the soldier. The collar tabs consisted of Guard lace in yellow gold on a white field

Above. German Marines wearing the Army-style dark-blue *Litewka* with the distinctive collar tabs. The dark-blue visorless field caps have a white band with the national cockade (*Reichskokarde*). Their shoulder-straps have an embroidered imperial crown over crossed anchors, with their battalion numbers in yellow thread

Right. German Marines, wearing khaki tunics without breast pockets, out on field maneuvers in the German colony of Kiautschou, China. Many have placed a band over the shako plates of their tropical helmets. The machine-gun crew is firing a Maxim MG-08 on a sled mount. In the distance is a gun crew carrying a machine gun in the field

Above left. During World War I the 1st and 2nd Sea Battalions served on the Western Front. They quickly adopted the Army's field uniforms based on the Model 1910 Service Tunic and the 1915 Field Blouse. The only distinctions from the uniforms of regular Army personnel were their collar tabs, shoulder-strap, and the white band with a single *Reichskokarde* on their caps

Above. Marines serving in tropical climates wore uniforms similar to those worn by colonial troops. However, there were differences in the style and cut, as well as the insignia. Note that his khaki tunic was made without breast pockets. He is wearing a shako plate on his tropical helmet

Left. A German Marine NCO of the 3rd Sea Battalion wearing musician's wings on his shoulders

Right. General Graf von Waldersee led the East Asia Brigade during the Boxer Rebellion of 1900–1. Here he is wearing the khaki uniform used by the German Expeditionary Forces. Of particular interest is his field cap, which shows very strong British influence, though with a *Reichskokarde* on the right side

Below. A bicycle troop from the 1st East Asia Brigade. They are wearing straw hats with the brim turned up and, attached to the side, the *Reichskokarde*, with the *Landeskokarde* immediately below it. Note the shoulder-strap with the numeral "1"

Below right. Members of the East Asia Brigade wearing the simple lightweight fatigue blouses and straw hats with *Reichskokarde*. Their stacked weapons are Gewehr 1898 Rifles

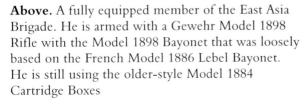

Above. A fully equipped member of the East Asia Brigade. He is armed with a Gewehr Model 1898 Rifle with the Model 1898 Bayonet that was loosely based on the French Model 1886 Lebel Bayonet. He is still using the older-style Model 1884 Cartridge Boxes

Above right. Prussian infantrymen of the East Asia Brigade preparing to be sent to China. In this excellent study of the field equipment used at the time of the Boxer Rebellion, the soldiers are all wearing the black leather Model 1895/1897 *Pickelhauben*. In 1895 a ventilator hole behind the spike base of the enlisted man's spiked helmet was added, and the use of both the national and state cockades became mandatory in 1897

Right. The black band with red piping around his tropical helmet identifies this soldier as an artillery-man. He is armed with the carbine version of the Gewehr Model 1898 Rifle (Kar. 98a) and a Model 1889 Cavalry Sword. Note the marksman lanyard on his *Litewka*

Above. This infantryman, as designated by the white band around his tropical helmet, is carrying the newer model cartridge pouch for the Mauser Rifle, adopted in 1898. Note the imperial German eagle plate on his tropical helmet. He is wearing the four-pocket field-grey *Litewka* with a concealed-button front flap down his tunic

Above. A review of the Allied forces in China by German and Russian officials. Of particular interest is the side view of the tropical helmets worn by the German infantrymen, with the white band and *Reichskokarde* affixed to the right side. The imperial Russian on the far left is armed with a Model 1891 Mosin-Nagant Rifle

Above. Imperial German engineers of the East Asia Brigade waiting to be sent to the field. Note how the long shovel is a part of their kit. Most are wearing just the *Reichskokarde* on their tropical helmets

Above. Members of the 1st East Asia Brigade wearing various styles of *Litewka* and headgear

Below. Members of the 2nd East Asia Brigade in khaki and field-grey *Litewkas*. The unique field-grey wool-covered leather *Pickelhaube*, made specially for the German Expeditionary Force to China, can be seen being worn by the soldier in the field-grey *Litewka* second from right. Note the musician's wings of the soldier standing to the rear of the group

Above. A group photograph of infantry and field artillery NCOs of the 2nd East Asia Brigade. Some of the artillerymen have black shoulder-straps with red piping and a chain-stitched script "F" on the straps. Note the distinctive cap bands – white and black with red piping – that designated the appropriate branches of service. The NCOs on the far right have the Model 1850 Artillery Officer's Swords, while the NCO second from left has a Saxon-style Officer's Sword

Below. An entourage of members of the East Asia Brigade and *Seebataillonen* watching German-raised Chinese troops fix bayonets to their Gewehr 1888 Rifles. Most of the obsolete equipment worn by the native troops, including the German-style belt-buckles and khaki uniforms, is of German origin. The uniforms worn by the Chinese soldiers are similar to those raised by the British (Her Majesty's 1st Chinese Regiment) during the Boxer Rebellion

Above left. This German senior NCO is serving with Turkish forces during World War I. He is wearing the German-influenced khaki uniform adopted by the Turkish Army. A former member of the *Schutztruppe*, he is wearing the imperial German ribbons for the Colonial Service and German Southwest Africa campaign medals. Note the distinctive Turkish helmet he is wearing: called a *kabalak*, it consists of a long cloth wound around a wickerwork base and resembles a sun helmet or solar topee

Above right. A German artillery officer serving with the Turkish Army. He is wearing the officer's version of the *kabalak* and the German-style Turkish officer's shoulder-boards. Note the flaming bombs device on his collars

Left. A German artilleryman serving in Palestine. He is wearing the Model 1915 Field Blouse and the tropical helmet with havelock. Note the imperial German helmet plate, the *Reichskokarde* on the side of the helmet and the distinctive black band with red piping for Artillery. He is armed with the Gewehr 1898 Rifle and the P.08 Automatic Pistol commonly known as the "Luger"

Above. Members of General Otto Liman von Sanders's Expeditionary Force to Palestine marching through the streets of Jerusalem. All are wearing khaki uniforms and tropical helmets with a large *Reichskokarde* on the front

Below. Another view of German troops in Palestine. Note the khaki visored field caps of the NCOs on the far right

Above. Burial of a comrade in the Holy Land. Note the various headgear worn by the German officers and enlisted men

Below. These two German soldiers are wearing lightweight khaki uniforms, and have adopted the standard headgear worn by the Arab population in Palestine

Right. Two enlisted men serving as field medics in Palestine. Both are wearing lightweight khaki uniforms and tropical helmets

Left. An enlisted member of a Guard Regiment serving in Palestine. Note the Guard's lace on the collars of his field-grey Model 1915 Field Blouse

Above. German troops serving in Macedonia. Most are wearing modified lightweight uniforms. Note the *Pickelhauben* covered with havelocks (*see inset*)

Right. German troops posing with a Bulgarian soldier on the Salonika Front. Many are wearing lightweight khaki uniforms based on the modified Model 1910 Tunics and the khaki field caps with havelocks of the type worn by the German Expeditionary Force in Palestine. Note the reissue of the Boxer Rebellion-era Straw Hats of the East Asia Brigade

Left. Of all the German troops that served overseas, General Lettow von Vorbeck's forces kept on fighting in German East Africa to the very end of the War and remained undefeated. In November 1918 he still had 1,500 active German troops and levies under his command. Still under arms, his *Schutztruppe* crossed the border into northern Rhodesia and surrendered a few days after the Armistice. He and his men were the only victorious army granted the privilege of marching through Berlin's Brandenburg Gate at the end of World War I. Seen here upon his return, many of his men are wearing a mixture of German and British headgear and uniforms. Note the distinctive white band for German East Africa on von Vorbeck's hat

Above. A veteran of the *Schutztruppe* wearing his Home Uniform Tunic in the 1930s. This former NCO had served in German East Africa. Many veterans continued to wear their uniforms at reunions, memorial services and special occasions

Above. When the veterans' uniforms were no longer serviceable or were lost, replicas of those worn by the *Schutztruppe* were made. This former member of the colonial troops is wearing the brown corduroy replica of the service uniform. As a member of a veterans' organization during the time of the Third Reich (1933–45), he was required to wear the armband of the Nazi Party. The badge below, adopted after World War I, was traditional of the German colonies. Known as the "*Kreuz des Südens*", the sleeve badge was also worn by selected German police units chosen to continue the "traditions" of the German police formations that served in the former colonies. In addition, a metal breast eagle of the German Veterans' League was pinned over the wearer's right pocket

3

WORLD WAR I
(1914–1918)

Above. War! German infantry marching to the front, August 1914. The men are wearing the Model 1910 Field Uniform and covers for their *Pickelhauben*. Note the NCO with Infantry Officer's Model Sword

Below. Prussian artillery officers and an NCO in a variety of greatcoats and headgear. The NCO at the far left is wearing the old dark-grey greatcoat that was introduced in 1867, while the officers are wearing stone-grey greatcoats, some with fur collars. Of particular interest is the shelter draped over with *zeltbahn* or shelter-half tents. Each soldier carried a shelter-half tent. It took two soldiers to make a tent, which they then shared

Above. A Prussian infantryman in full marching order wearing the Model 1910 Field Uniform in 1914. Note the Brandenburg-style cuffs. The twisted two-colored piping around his shoulder-straps indicates that he is a one-year volunteer (a scheme that was cancelled after 3 October 1914) for military service. His boots are the high-shaft natural leather enlisted men's Model 1866 Marching Boots

Above. A soldier wearing the Model 1910 Tunic with Swedish-style cuffs. He is wearing a cloth cover with unit designation over his spiked helmet. Note how the soldier's bayonet scabbard has been strapped to the shaft of his entrenching shovel

Left. Bavarian infantrymen wearing the Model 1910 Field Tunics with Brandenburg-style cuffs. The drummer is wearing musician's wings on his tunic. Because of limited supplies, substitutes or ersatz items began to appear, such as the felt *Pickelhauben* being worn by the soldiers. Note the difference between the black leather helmet worn by the musician and the ersatz felt helmets worn by the other soldiers

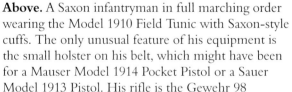

Above. A Saxon infantryman in full marching order wearing the Model 1910 Field Tunic with Saxon-style cuffs. The only unusual feature of his equipment is the small holster on his belt, which might have been for a Mauser Model 1914 Pocket Pistol or a Sauer Model 1913 Pistol. His rifle is the Gewehr 98

Above right. A Saxon NCO wearing the Model 1910 Field Uniform with Saxon-style cuffs. He has NCO braid on his collar and cuffs

Right. This soldier is wearing the shoulder-straps of a Saxon Regiment on his Model 1910 Field Uniform with Saxon-style cuffs, 1915. Note the ersatz *Pickelhaube* of pressed felt and without the metal visor trim

Above left. A Saxon Jäger wearing the distinctive shako with his Model 1910 Tunic with Saxon-style cuffs

Above. An NCO of the 24th Pioneer Battalion from the VII Army Corps District. Most pioneer units wore Swedish-style cuffs on their tunic and black piping on the shoulder-straps, cuffs, down the front of the tunic and on the field cap. He is wearing the 1910 Pattern Field Cap with his uniform. Note the collar disc for senior NCOs. He is armed with a P.08 (Luger) Pistol

Left. This Prussian infantryman is wearing the Modified Model 1910 Field Tunic that was introduced in 1915. Note the barrel cuffs that replaced the earlier and differing styles of cuffs. Of particular interest is the ersatz *Pickelhaube* made of metal and then painted field-grey. An ersatz Model 1915/16 Bayonet is fixed to his Gewehr 98

Right. This soldier is wearing the Model 1915 Field Blouse and the Model 1916 Steel Helmet that replaced the *Pickelhaube*. He has a gasmask hanging from his neck. Dog's hide was initially used for gasmasks since dogs do not perspire through their skin, which is therefore suitable for preventing harmful gas or chemicals from penetrating the mask. Manufactured materials such as rubberized canvas were used later on

Far right. This NCO is in full marching order. A German soldier was expected to carry a comparatively heavy load consisting of a belt, three cartridge pouches (two up front, one in the rear), knapsack, ration bag, greatcoat, mess-kit, haversack, canteen, entrenching tool and rifle. In addition, this NCO is carrying a map case and sword

Above. A group of soldiers wearing the Model 1908 Greatcoats introduced on 1 February 1908. The soldier in the background is wearing a Model 1893 *Litewka* with collar patches and a pre-War visored undress cap. The NCO on the far right is wearing the old pre-War dark-grey greatcoat. The soldiers are armed with Gewehr 1888 Rifles, while the NCO on the far left is armed with the Mauser Model 1896 "Broomhandle" Pistol

Left. A sentry wearing the grey Model 1908 Greatcoat. He is armed with the Gewehr 1888 Rifle with Model 1871 Bayonet

Right. A foot artilleryman wearing the Model 1910 Field Tunic with Brandenburg-style cuffs. He is armed with a Gewehr 91, a variation of the Karabiner 88 and of its parent, the Gewehr 1888 Commission Rifle. In Prussia, and later in the other states of the Reich, foot artillery were equipped with 91 Rifles. Most were made by the Suhl manufacturers V. C. Schilling and C. G. Haenel, since the state factories were busy filling orders for the Gewehr 1888 Infantry Rifles. By 1892, these manufacturers had delivered a total of some 200,000 carbines to Prussia, Saxony, Württemburg and Bavaria

Above. German soldiers serving in the Carpathian Mountains wearing heavy sheepskin winter coats over their uniforms and equipment (as evidenced by the bulges in their coats). Most have a gasmask can strung from their necks and are armed with an assortment of weapons, from Gewehr 98 Rifles to Stick Grenades

Above left. An artilleryman of the 22nd Field Artillery from Münster wearing the Model 1910 Field Tunic with Swedish-style cuffs. His field-grey peakless field cap has the black band with red piping. Note the flaming bomb emblem over his regimental number on his shoulder-straps

Above. A Prussian Hussar wearing the field-grey Model 1910 *Attila*. His busby has a cover permitting his cockade to be shown. Since 1889 troopers from all the Hussar Regiments were armed with a lance, the shaft of which was wood for the Saxon Regiments and steel for the Prussian and Brunswick Regiments

Left. A Hussar from the 1st Life Hussar Regiment wearing the field-grey Model 1910 *Attila*. Note how the field cover of his ersatz busby of pressed felt has been lifted up and is supported by the cockade, revealing the distinctive regimental plate. He is armed with the Gewehr 98 Rifle with an ersatz Model 1915/16 Bayonet

Above left. During the years of the War, the field-grey Hussar uniform was used as a walking-out uniform. Note the field cap and pre-War riding boots with distinctive white trim

Above. An Oberleutnant of the 17th Brunswick Hussar Regiment wearing the distinctive regimental badge on his field-grey undress cap

Left. Crown Prince Wilhelm, Commander of the 5th Army, with the regimental insignia of the 1st Life Hussar Regiment on his pre-War undress cap. He is wearing a tailored field-grey officer field tunic with four patch pockets. The pattern was similar in style to those worn by the Württemberg Ski and Mountain Troops. A few aristocrats and senior officers had specially tailored uniforms made that occasionally conflicted with uniform regulations. Rank does have its privileges

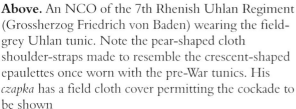

Above. An NCO of the 7th Rhenish Uhlan Regiment (Grossherzog Friedrich von Baden) wearing the field-grey Uhlan tunic. Note the pear-shaped cloth shoulder-straps made to resemble the crescent-shaped epaulettes once worn with the pre-War tunics. His *czapka* has a field cloth cover permitting the cockade to be shown

Above right. Three members of an Uhlan Regiment. The one in the center is wearing a lightweight drill jacket modeled on a *Litewka*, while the other two are wearing the Model 1910 Uhlan Tunics. Note that the soldier on the far left is wearing the normal shoulder-straps instead of the distinctive Uhlan pear-shaped shoulder-straps. The soldier on the far right is wearing the "camouflage" grey band on the lower part of his *feldmütze*, which nonetheless allows his national cockade to be shown

Right. The era of horses and men in combat are long gone, and this Uhlan is now reduced to fighting from a trench as an infantryman. He is wearing the Model 1916 Steel Helmet with his Model 1910 Uhlan Tunic

Left. A Bavarian Dragoon wearing the Model 1910 Tunic with Swedish-style cuffs. His ersatz *Pickelhaube* is made of metal and no longer has the squared front visor normally worn by Bavarian troops since its adoption in 1886. He has the NCO's and trooper's Pattern "Pallasch" Sword attached to his saddle

Below. German cavalrymen from a Dragoon Regiment in full rig. Note the Gewehr 98 Rifles in their leather carriers. All are wearing the Dragoon-style *Pickelhaube* with squared visor and cloth cover

Opposite above. Train troops (*Eisenbahntruppen*) wearing the Model 1893 *Litewka* with the script "E" on their shoulder-straps. Many are armed with Gewehr 1888 Rifles and Model 1871 Bayonets

Opposite below. French prisoners of war being led by a Gendarmerie of the Prussian Guard Regiment and guarded by a detachment of infantrymen from the 118th Regiment. Their regimental designations are clearly visible on their *Pickelhaube* covers. The soldiers are armed with Gewehr 1898 Rifles fixed with the Model 1898n/A Bayonet

Above. Soldiers of the 2nd Guards Railway Troops Regiment. All have double *Kapellenlitzen* on the collar and cuffs of their Model 1910 Field Uniforms, and are wearing the distinctive Model 1915 Field Caps with black leather chin-straps that were usually issued to supply and medical personnel. The shoulder-boards have a scripted "E" over a "2"

Left. A soldier from the Prussian 6th Jäger Regiment wearing the Model 1860/95 Shako and Model 1910 Field Tunic with Swedish-style cuffs. He has a scripted "J" over a "6" on his shoulder-straps

Right. NCOs from the 5th Jäger Regiment wearing covers that permit the shako's cockade to be shown. The stenciled unit numeral on the shako cover can clearly be seen being worn by the soldier on the left. Note the use of puttees and leather gaiters

Above. Soldiers from a Prussian Jäger unit wearing the ersatz 1915 Pattern Shakos of pressed felt

Below. An unidentified Prussian Jäger detachment patrolling the streets of Brussels in 1915. All the men are wearing covers for their shakos with the state cockade visible (white and black), and are armed with Gewehr 1898 Rifles

Left. An NCO from a Guard unit wearing a Model 1916 Steel Helmet and armed with a P.08 (Luger) Pistol

Right. Karl Heidenreich as a soldier of the 5th Reserve-Jägerbataillon (Hirschberg), wearing the distinctive insignia of the Karpathenkorps on his field cap

Below. Members of a Pioneer unit dressed in a combination of Model 1910 and Model 1910/15 Field Uniforms. The soldiers are using the straps from their breadbags to support the load from their cartridge pouches. Note the use of the Model 1893 Ankleboots and the Model 1866 Marching Boots. Note how the soldier on the far right has tucked his pant legs into his socks. All are armed with the Karabiner 98a

Above left. An enlisted man wearing the Karpathen-korps and Edelweiss insignia on his *feldmütze*. The metal "S" pinned to the collar of his Model 1915 Field Blouse identifies him as a member of the 1st Bavarian Ski Battalion

Above. Bavarian Ski Troops wore a modified Model 1915 Field Blouse with the addition of two breast-patch pockets. Note the "S" collar patches being worn by the soldier on the right (*see inset*)

Left. A soldier of a Württemberg Ski Company, 1915–16. Note the mountain cap (*Gebirgsmutze*), based on those worn by Austrian Mountain Troops (*see inset*). A certain Oberleutnant by the name of Erwin Rommel served with the Württemberg Mountain Battalion while campaigning in the Transylvanian Alps

Left. These artillerymen, as denoted by the flaming bomb devices on their shoulder-straps, are wearing the modified Model 1910 Field Tunics (Model 1910/15). Note the use of the *Gebirgsmütze*, possibly signifying an affiliation with a mountain troop unit

Right. Prior to 1915 most priests serving as chaplains wore their traditional habits with a violet armband identifying their status as non-combatants. This chaplain is wearing a black frock coat and *feldmütze*

Above. These recaptured German prisoners of war had been caught by the Americans as they were trying to return to their lines. The one on the left is wearing the German Army-issue undershirt, while the one on the right is wearing the Model 1895 Fatigue Jacket of twilled linen

Above right. An NCO wearing the gorget of the Gardes du Corps Regiment with his Model 1910 Tunic

Right. An excellent study of the differences between the Model 1910 and the modified Model 1910/15 Tunics, as well as the Field Caps

Left. In 1915 the Army introduced a special uniform for military chaplains. This Catholic priest – as denoted by his crucifix – is wearing the long field-grey chaplain's frock coat and hat. Note the lack of any rank insignia on the uniform, and the cross between the cockades on his colonial-style hat. The violet armband is retained with the uniform

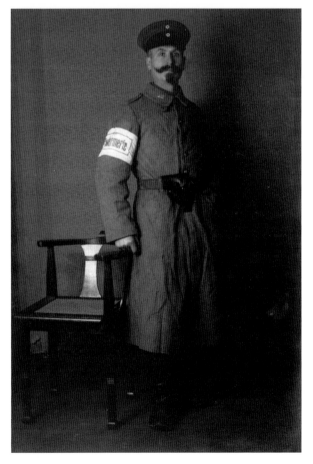

Above left. An Obergendarm of the Feldgendarmerie or Military Police. The Military Police were made up of seconded Prussian Rural Police (Landgendarmerie) personnel and cavalry troopers. They wore dark-green Model 1889 Tunics, Dragoon-style *Pickelhauben* and a silver gorget. An Oberwachtmeister had two cuff braids and an Obergendarmen a yellow loop attached to the shoulder-board

Above. Two members of the Feldgendarmerie on duty. Note the use of the Swedish-style and Polish-style cuffs. Of particular interest is the Prussian eagle at each end of the gorget, either side of the soldier's personal number. Felgendarmerie from other states had the following: Bavaria – coat of arms with lion's heads at each corner; Saxony – coat of arms; Württemberg – coat of arms. Those serving in a Reserve Corps sported an "R" in addition to the personal number

Left. A Landsturmmann serving as a temporary Feldgendarm. Note the armband with "Gendarmerie" worn on the greatcoat

Above. An NCO wearing the Medical Personnel (Sanitätsunterpersonal) Arm Badge on his Model 1915 Field Blouse

Above right. The Totenkopf Unit Traditions Badge was also worn by the 92nd Brunswick Infantry Regiment, as can be seen on their field caps. Note the Red Cross armband being worn by the stretcher bearer

Right. Another soldier serving as a temporary Feldgendarm. He is wearing an armband with "Hilfsgendarmerie" on his field blouse

Above. A Group of senior NCOs from the 395th Infantry Regiment of the 18th Reserve Infantry Brigade. Note the double sleeve rings of the three holding the position of "*Der Spiess*"

Below. A member of an Airship Detachment (Luftschiffer-Abteilung) in pre-War uniform. Note the script "L" over "4" on his shoulder-strap

Below. This NCO from an Airship Detachment is firing a Maxim MG-08 Machine Gun

Right.
Members of the 1st Machine Gun Company of the 209th Infantry Regiment posing with a balloon. Note the MG-08 Machine Guns

Left. The winged propeller on this NCO's shoulder-strap identifies him as a member of a Flying Battalion. He is wearing the Model 1860/95 Shako and Model 1910 Tunic with Swedish-style cuffs. Note the Guard's double *Kapellenlitzen* on the collar and cuffs, and the marksmanship lanyard and wound badge in silver

Below. A soldier of the 228th Flying Battalion. We can see his shoulder-strap with the Aviation insignia worn on the Model 1915 Field Blouse

Above left. A German aviator in full rig, consisting of sheepskin-lined greatcoat, leather gloves, Model 1913 Goggles, leather flying helmet and Model 1913 Motor Transport Corps Crash Helmet

Above. A Leutnant wearing the field-grey Model 1910 Officer's Service Tunic. Note the Observer's Badge

Left. A Leutnant wearing a privately modified Model 1910 Officer's Tunic with additional breast-patch pockets. Note the Pilot's Badge

Above. NCOs of a Flying Battalion wearing a wide assortment of greatcoats of various shades and quality. All have the winged propeller on their shoulder-straps

Left. Hans Bauer wearing a modified Model 1915 Field Blouse with patch pockets similar to those worn by the Ski Troops. He is wearing officer-quality Guard-style double-*Kapellenlitzen* collar tabs, but no rank shoulder-boards. Note the Bavarian Pilot's Badge. Hans Bauer became Adolf Hitler's personal pilot in the decades following World War I

Right. Throughout the War the Model 1893 *Litewka* continued to be worn by some soldiers. By 1915 it influenced the creation of the field-grey Model 1915 Field Blouse. This artillery-man from a Guard Regiment is wearing a *Litewka* with pockets, showing the many differing styles that can be found with this jacket. Note the knot attached to the bayonet frog of his Model 1884/98 Dress Bayonet

Above left. An NCO of a Landsturm Infantry Battalion wearing the Model 1915 Field Blouse. The Landsturm was established during the Napoleonic Wars as a paramilitary unit to support the German Army when the homeland was threatened. During World War I many Landsturm Infantry Battalions were assigned to Reserve and Landwehr Infantry Regiments. The numbers of the parent infantry brigade were worn on the collar. In April 1915 it was replaced with the corps number above the battalion number

Above. The numerals (III B/10) on the collar of this Landsturmmann identify him as a soldier of the 10th Landsturm Battalion of the 3rd Bavarian Army Corps. He is wearing an ersatz 1915 Pattern *Pickelhaube* of pressed felt and the modified Model 1910/15 Tunic. Breadbag straps are used to hold his cartridge pouches and belt in place. He is armed with a captured and reissued Russian Model 1891 Mosin-Nagant Rifle

Left. A member of the 8th Landsturm Infantry Battalion of the 16th Army Corps wearing a Model 1915 Field Blouse. He is armed with a Russian Model 1891 Mosin-Nagant Rifle modified to accept an ersatz Model 1916 Bayonet

Above. Men of the 102nd Landsturm Infantry Battalion wearing the distinctive Model 1813 oilcloth peaked caps bearing the Landwehr Cross above the state cockade. All are wearing the Model 1893 *Litewka* and are armed with the Karabiner 98a Rifle

Below. Soldiers with the 57th Landsturm Infantry Battalion wearing the Model 1860 Shako and Model 1910 Tunic with Brandenburg-style cuffs. The distinctive Landwehr Cross can be seen on the shako. All are armed with the Gewehr 1888 Rifle. Note the musician's wings worn by the bugler on the far left

Left. Two soldiers from the Landwehr Infantry serving as temporary Feldgendarmerie. Both are armed with the Gewehr 1888 Rifle

Above. An early war scene showing a Maxim MG-08 Machine-Gun Crew from the 106th Infantry Regiment. Note the Luger of the kneeling soldier holding the binoculars

Below. A late war scene of a machine-gun crew. Note the mixture of uniforms and headgear. Most are wearing on their left sleeve the Machine Gunner's Marksmen Sleeve Badges that were introduced on 19 February 1916. Some of the men are wearing a field-grey band over the red band of their field caps

Above. Bavarian cooks preparing a meal for the troops in a mobile field kitchen or *gulaschkanonen*. All are wearing the off-white Model 1895 Drill/Fatigue Uniform made of herringbone twill

Below. A crewman sits next to German A7V Tank "Adalbert", which took a total of eighteen men. It carried a 57-mm gun and seven machine guns. A Tank Crew Badge was authorized at the end of the War. "Adalbert" went through various actions and was finally captured by the French after the Armistice

Left. A German soldier demonstrates a captured French flame thrower used to clear pillboxes and trenches

Right. An officer of a Guard Regiment wearing the Model 1910 Officer's Field Uniform

Above. Three officers out in the field. One is a member of the 92nd Brunswick Infantry Regiment. Note the tent made from various *zeltbahn*, and field equipment hanging from the trees

Above left. A Leutnant wearing the regimental insignia of the 25th Dragoon Regiment on his shoulder-board

Above. This general is wearing the Model 1910 General Officer's Field Tunic with breast pockets, Model 1900 "Alt-Larisch" Collar Tabs, and barrel cuffs

Left. An officer wearing the Model 1903 Officer's Undress Tunic *Litewka* with colored collar patch and the Model 1910 Peaked Field Cap

Above. An excellent view of the field marshal's shoulder-board, worn by Prince Leopold while reviewing Saxon Jäger and infantry troops

Left. Field Marshal Emil von Eichhorn wearing the Model 1903 Officer's Undress *Litewka* with colored patch and gold buttons

Right. A full view of a general wearing the Model 1910 General Officer's Field Tunic

Above. A group of Prussian general officers wearing their stone-grey Model 1903 General Officer's Greatcoats with red lapels

Below. A field marshal, senior officers and foreign dignitaries reviewing troops of a Guard Regiment, 1917

Left. A close-up of the previous photograph showing an excellent array of uniforms. Amongst the group is an officer of the *Schutztruppe*, Feldgendarmerie with their distinctive gorgets, Saxon Jäger, Cuirassier, Dragoon, Uhlan, Austrian, Bulgarian and Turkish officers

Below. War came to an end on the eleventh hour of the eleventh day of the eleventh month of 1918. These soldiers taken prisoner by the American Expeditionary Force show the condition of the German Army at the Western Front after fighting for well over four years

Bottom. The horrors of war. Much of this soldier's personal equipment is scattered about his remains – his Gewehr 98 Rifle, Model 1910 Mess-Tin, Model 1893 Water Bottle, Model 1892 Shelter-Quarter (*zeltbahn*), Model 1916 Steel Helmet, Model 1909 Cartridge Pouches, Model 1915 Gasmask and Model 1898/05 Bayonet

UNIFORM PLATES
OF THE
IMPERIAL GERMAN ARMY

Illustrations from p. 155 to p. 160 are from *Die Deutsche Armee vor dem Weltkriege*.
Leipzig: Verlag von Moritz Ruhl, 1926

Illustrations from p. 161 to p. 162 are from *Das Kleine Buch vom Deutschen Heere*.
Kiel & Leipzig: Verlag von Lipsius & Tischer, 1901

Above. Prussia: Garde du Corps (infantry and cavalry)

Below. Prussia: infantry

Above. Prussia: Cuirassiers (Heavy Cavalry), Dragoons, and Jäger zu Pferde (Mounted Rifles)

Below. Prussia: Hussars and Uhlans (Lancers)

Above. Prussia: artillery, Pioneers, train and transport troops

Below. Prussia: Gendarmerie (Military Police), staff orderlies, cadets, military school administration staff

Above. Prussia: medical doctors, military administration officials, etc.

Below. Mecklenburg – Oldenburg – Braunschweig

Above. Baden – Hessen

Below. Bavaria

Above. Saxony

Below. Württemberg

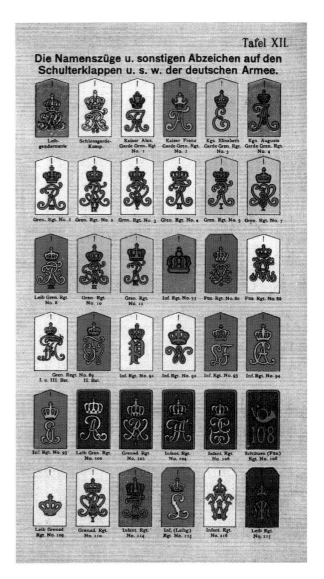

Above. Officers' insignia (epaulettes and shoulder-boards)

Above. Distinctive regimental emblems on shoulder-straps of the German Army

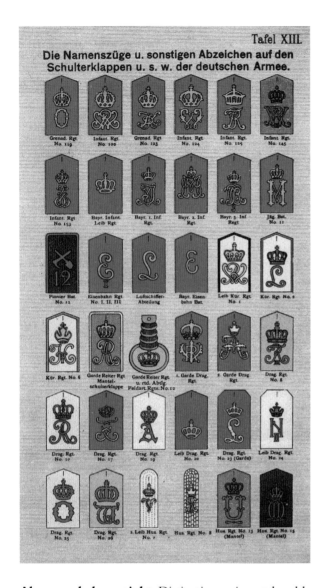

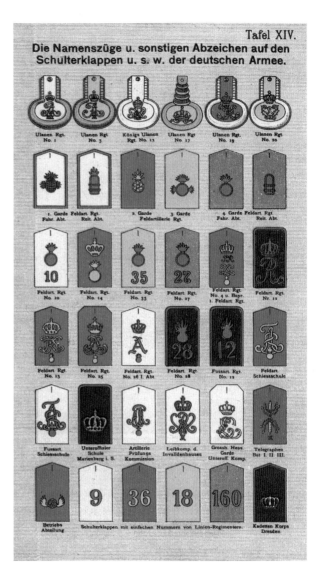

Above and above right. Distinctive regimental emblems on shoulder-straps of the German Army

APPENDIX

UNIFORM PLATES
OF THE
IMPERIAL GERMAN
COLONIAL TROOPS

Illustrations from p. 165 to the top of page p. 168 are from *Die Ehemaligen Kaiserlich Deutschen Schutztruppen*. Leipzig: Verlag von Moritz Ruhl, 1910

Schutztruppe für Südwestafrika.

| Offiziere. | | | | Soldat. | Hornist. | Unter- |
| im Mantel. | Parade-Anzug. | Kl Dienst-Anzug. | Feld-Anzug. | Dienst-Anzug. | Ausgeh-Anzug. | Büchsenmacher.
Ordonnanz-Anzug. |

Above and below. *Schutztruppe* for German Southwest Africa

Schutztruppe für Südwestafrika.

| Arzt. | Lazarethgehilfen. | | Unteroffizier. | Rossarzt. | Zahlmeister. | Feldwebel. |
| Kl Dienst-Anzug. | im Mantel. | Ordonn-Anzug. | Ausgeh-Anzug. | Parade-Anzug. | Dienst-Anzug. | Kl.Dienst-Anzug. | Ausgeh-Anzug. |

Schutztruppe für Ostafrika.

| Zahlmeister. | Offiziere. | | Aerzte. | Lazarethgehilfe | Sergeant. |
| Dienst-Anzug. | Parade-Anzug. | Kleiner Dienst-Anzug. | im Mantel. | Ordonnanz-Anzug. | |

Above and below. *Schutztruppe* for German East Africa

Schutztruppe für Ostafrika.

Feldwebel.	Zahlmeister-Aspirant.	Ober-Feuerwerker.	Ober-	Unter-	Unteroffiziere.	Sudanese.
Ordonnanz-Anzug.	Ausgeh-Anzug.		Büchsenmacher.		im Mantel. Ordonnanz-Anzug	
			Ordonn.-Anzug. Ausgeh-Anzug.			

Schutztruppe für Kamerun und Togo.

| Zahlmeister. Kl Dienst-Anzug. | Zahlmeister-Aspirant. Ausgeh-Anzug. | Ober-Feuerwerker. | Arzt. Dienst-Anzug. | Offiziere. Dienst-Anzug. Kl Dienst-Anzug. | Unteroffizier Gefreiter. Ausgeh-Anzug. |

Above. *Schutztruppe* for German Cameroon and Togo   **Below.** Rank and other insignia

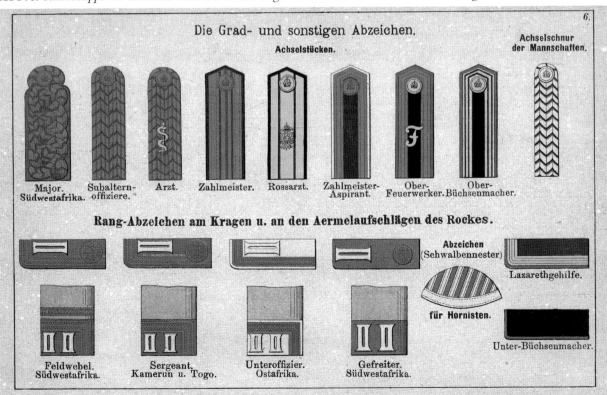

Die Grad- und sonstigen Abzeichen.

Achselstücken.

Achselschnur der Mannschaften.

| Major. Südwestafrika. | Subaltern-offiziere. | Arzt. | Zahlmeister. | Rossarzt. | Zahlmeister-Aspirant. | Ober-Feuerwerker. | Ober-Büchsenmacher. |

Rang-Abzeichen am Kragen u. an den Aermelaufschlägen des Rockes.

Abzeichen (Schwalbennester)

für Hornisten.

Lazarethgehilfe.

Unter-Büchsenmacher.

| Feldwebel. Südwestafrika. | Sergeant. Kamerun u. Togo. | Unteroffizier. Ostafrika. | Gefreiter. Südwestafrika. |

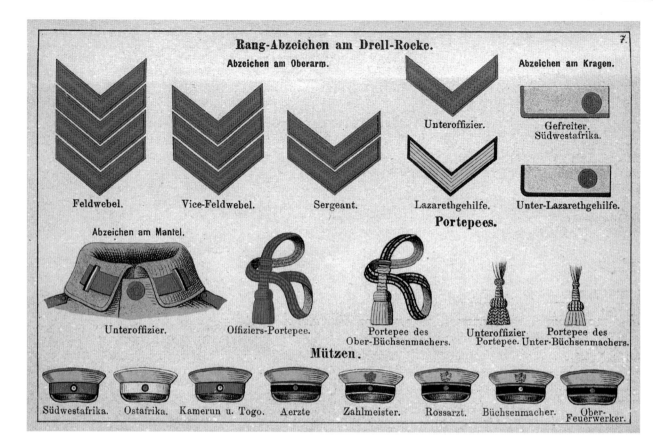

Above. Rank insignia, portepees and caps

Below. A turn-of-the-nineteenth-century illustration showing uniforms of the Naval Sea Battalion and colonial troops in German East Africa

UNIFORM PLATES
OF THE
IMPERIAL GERMAN ARMY
DURING WORLD WAR I

Illustrations are from *Die Graue Felduniform der Deutschen Armee*.
Leipzig: Verlag von Moritz Ruhl, 1910

Die graue Felduniform der Offiziere.

General.   Oberst vom   Garde-Infant.-   Infanterie-Offizier.   Jäger-Offizier.   Garde-Pionier-   Pionier-   1. G.-Maschinengew.-Abt.
Generalstabe.   Offizier.   21. Armeekorps   Offizier.   Offizier.   Offizier.

Die graue Felduniform der Offiziere.

R. Gardes du Corps.   Kürassier-   Dragoner-   Husaren-   Feldartillerie-   Jäger z. Pferde.   Garde-Train   Garde-Ulanen-
Offizier.   Offizier.   Offizier.   Offizier.   Offizier.   Offizier   Offizier.   Offizier.
   7. Kür.-R.   12. Drag.-R   16. Hus.-R   v. 2. R. Jäg. z. Pf.

9.

Die graue Felduniform der Offiziere.

| Bayer. Inf.-Leib-R. Offizier. | Bayer. Jäger-Offizier. | Bayer. Ulanen-Offizier. | Chevauleger-Offizier 4. Chevaul.-R. | Sächs. Leib-Gren.-R. 100 Offizier. | Sächs. Schützen-Reg. 108 Offizier. | Sächs. Fussartillerie. Offizier. | Sächs. G.-Reiter-R. Offizier. |

4.

Die graue Felduniform der Sanitätsoffiziere u. s. w., sowie der Militärbeamten.

| Zahlmeister. | Feuerwerks-Offizier. | Sanitäts-Offizier. | Veterinär-Offizier. | Festungsbau-Offizier. | Proviantverwltgs-Beamter. | Kriegsgerichtsrat. Wirkl. Geh. Kriegsrat. | Intendantur-Beamter. |

II.

Die graue Felduniform der Mannschaften.

1.

5. Garde-Gren.-R.   3. Garde-Feldart.-R.   Garde-Pionier-Bat.   Garde-Schützen-Bat.

4. Garde-Reg. z. Fuss.   Garde-Train-Bat.   Garde-Jäger-Bat.   2. Garde-Maschinengew.
Sergeant   Abteilung.

II.

Die graue Felduniform der Mannschaften.

2.

Infanterie IV. A.-K.   Infanterie VIII. A.-K.   10. Jäger-Bat.   Infant.-R. 114.

Infanterie II. A.-K.   Hornist   Infanterie V. A.-K.   7. Maschinengew.-Abt.   Krankenträger.   Unteroffizier
Gren.-R 2.   I.-R. 26.   Feldwebel I.-R. 58.

Die graue Felduniform der Mannschaften.

Gardes du Corps. Feldart.-I.-A.-K. Gefreiter Leib-Garde-Hus.-R. 5. Kür.-R. 6. Hus.-R. 13. Hus.-R. 7. Fussart.-R. 13. Pion.-Bat.

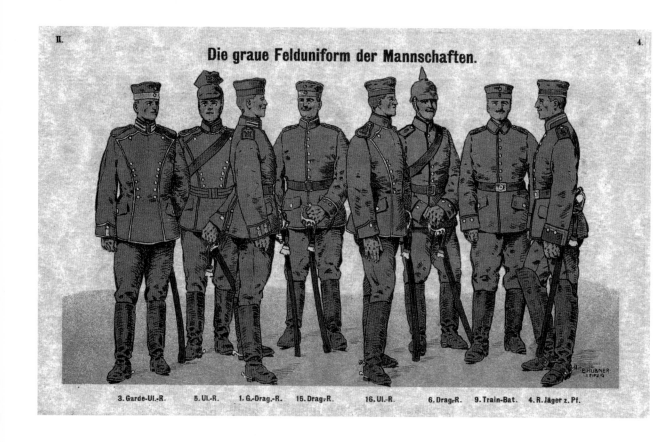

Die graue Felduniform der Mannschaften.

3. Garde-Ul.-R. 5. Ul.-R. 1. G.-Drag.-R. 15. Drag.-R. 16. Ul.-R. 6. Drag.-R. 9. Train-Bat. 4. R. Jäger z. Pf.

Die graue Felduniform der Mannschaften - Sächsische Truppenteile.

Infanterie XIX. A.-K.   Infanterie XII. A.-K.   21. Ul.-R.   Fussartillerie.   Pionier.
2. Jäger-Bat. Unteroffizier Schützen-R. 108. Leibgr.-R. 100. Karab.-R.   Train.   18. Hus.-R.   Feldart. XII. A.-K.
                                                                                 Gefreiter

Die graue Felduniform der Mannschaften - Bayerische Truppenteile.

        Jäger   Infanterie   1. Ul.-R.   Fussartillerie.   Pionier. 1. schw. Reiter-R.
Infanterie - Leib-R.   II. A.-K.   III. A.-K.   3. Chevauleger-R.   Train. Feldart. III. A.-K.

Waffenröcke etc.

II.

Waffenrock mit Klappkragen.

Vorderseite
(hier 4. Garde-R. z. F.)

Rückseite
(Inf.-Rgt.)

Waffenrock mit Stehkragen.
(hier 8. Kür.-Rgt.)

Vorderseite

Rückseite

Attila.

Achselklappen.

7.

Infanterie.

Kürassiere.

Ulanen.

Husaren.

Jäger zu Pferde.

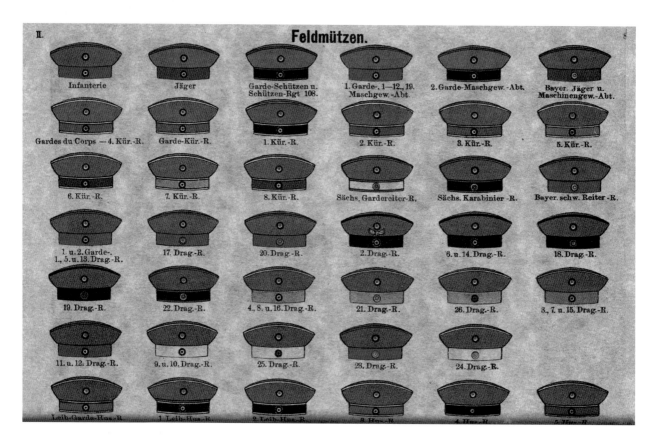

Feldmützen.

II.

Infanterie

Jäger

Garde-Schützen u.
Schützen-Rgt. 108.

1. Garde-, 1—12., 19.
Maschgew.-Abt.

2. Garde-Maschgew.-Abt.

Bayer. Jäger u.
Maschinengew.-Abt.

Gardes du Corps — 4. Kür.-R.

Garde-Kür.-R.

1. Kür.-R.

2. Kür.-R.

3. Kür.-R.

5. Kür.-R.

6. Kür.-R.

7. Kür.-R.

8. Kür.-R.

Sächs. Gardereiter-R.

Sächs. Karabinier-R.

Bayer. schw. Reiter-R.

1. u. 2. Garde-,
1., 5. u. 13. Drag.-R.

17. Drag.-R.

20. Drag.-R.

2. Drag.-R.

6. u. 14. Drag.-R.

18. Drag.-R.

19. Drag.-R.

22. Drag.-R.

4., 8. u. 16. Drag.-R.

21. Drag.-R.

26. Drag.-R.

3., 7. u. 15. Drag.-R.

11. u. 12. Drag.-R.

9. u. 10. Drag.-R.

25. Drag.-R.

23. Drag.-R.

24. Drag.-R.

Leib-Garde-Hus.-R.

1. Leib-Hus.-R.

2. Leib-Hus.-R.

3. Hus.-R.

4. Hus.-R.

5. Hus.-R.

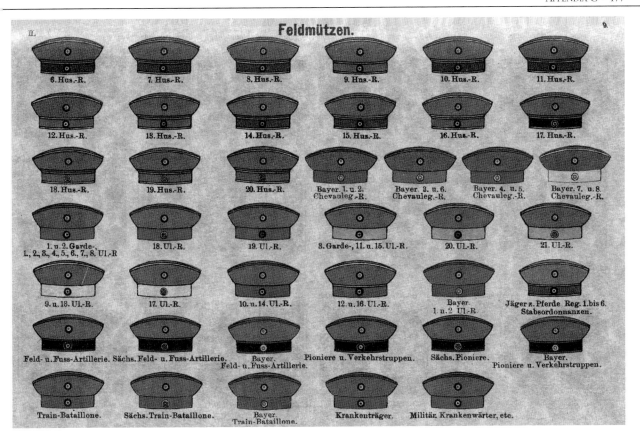

Feldmützen.

II.

6. Hus.-R.	7. Hus.-R.	8. Hus.-R.	9. Hns.-R.	10. Hus.-R.	11. Hus.-R.
12. Hus.-R.	13. Hus.-R.	14. Hus.-R.	15. Hus.-R.	16. Hus.-R.	17. Hus.-R.
18. Hus.-R.	19. Hus.-R.	20. Hus.-R.	Bayer. 1. u. 2. Chevauleg.-R.	Bayer. 3. u. 6. Chevauleg.-R.	Bayer. 4. u. 5. Chevauleg.-R.	Bayer. 7. u. 8. Chevauleg.-R.
1. u. 2. Garde-, 1., 2., 3., 4., 5., 6., 7., 8. Ul-R	18. Ul.-R.	19. Ul.-R.	3. Garde-, 11. u. 15. Ul.-R.	20. Ul.-R.	21. Ul.-R.
9. u. 13. Ul.-R.	17. Ul.-R.	10. u. 14. Ul.-R.	12. u. 16. Ul.-R.	Bayer. 1. u. 2 Ul.-R.	Jäger z. Pferde Reg. 1. bis 6. Stabsordonnanzen.
Feld- u. Fuss-Artillerie.	Sächs. Feld- u. Fuss-Artillerie.	Bayer. Feld- u. Fuss-Artillerie.	Pioniere u. Verkehrstruppen.	Sächs. Pioniere.	Bayer. Pioniere u. Verkehrstruppen.
Train-Bataillone.	Sächs. Train-Bataillone.	Bayer. Train-Bataillone.	Krankenträger.	Militär. Krankenwärter, etc.	

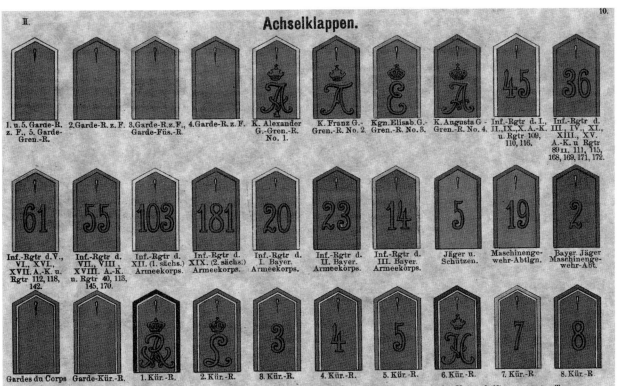

Achselklappen.

II.

1. u. 5. Garde-R. z. F., 5. Garde-Gren.-R.	2. Garde-R. z. F.	3. Garde-R. z. F., Garde-Füs.-R.	4. Garde-R. z. F.	K. Alexander G.-Gren.-R. No. 1.	K. Franz G.-Gren.-R. No. 2	Kgn. Elisab. G.-Gren.-R. No. 3.	K. Augusta G.-Gren.-R. No. 4.	Inf.-Rgtr d. I., II., IX., X. A.-K. u. Rgtr 109, 110, 116.	Inf.-Rgtr d. III., IV., XI., XIII., XV. A.-K. u Rgtr 89 u. 111, 115, 168, 169, 171, 172.
61	55	103	181	20	23	14	5	19	2
Inf.-Rgtr d. V., VI., XVI., XVII. A.-K. u. Rgtr 112, 118, 142.	Inf.-Rgtr d. VII., VIII., XVIII. A.-K. u. Rgtr 40, 118, 145, 170.	Inf.-Rgtr d. XII. (1. sächs.) Armeekorps.	Inf.-Rgtr d. XIX. (2. sächs.) Armeekorps.	Inf.-Rgtr d. I. Bayer. Armeekorps.	Inf.-Rgtr d. II. Bayer. Armeekorps.	Inf.-Rgtr d. III. Bayer. Armeekorps.	Jäger u. Schützen.	Maschinenge-wehr-Abtlgn,	Bayer. Jäger Maschinenge-wehr-Abt.
Gardes du Corps	Garde-Kür.-R.	1. Kür.-R.	2. Kür.-R.	3. Kür.-R.	4. Kür.-R.	5. Kür.-R.	6. Kür.-R.	7. Kür.-R.	8. Kür.-R

In den dargestellten Achselklappen konnte natürlich nur immer eine Nummer oder ein Abzeichen von den in den Unterschriften genannten Truppen-tellen angegeben werden — Die Namenszüge sind dieselben, wie solche in dem I. Teil des Werkes: „Die Uniformen der Deutschen Armee" dargestellt

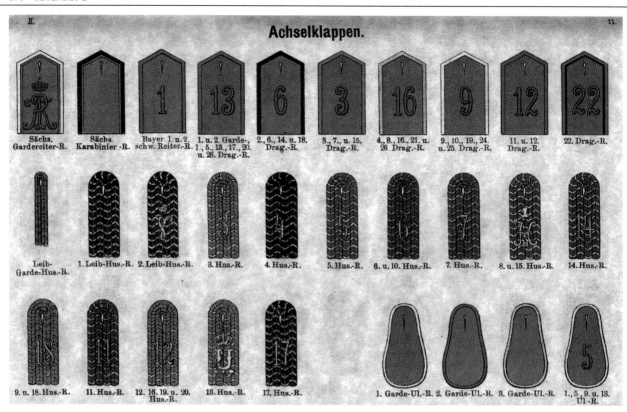

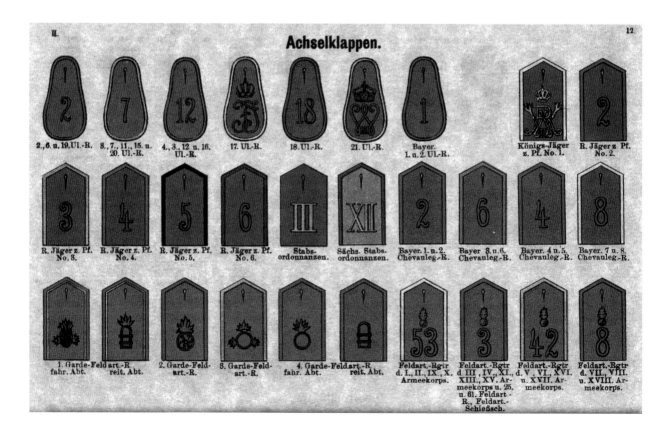

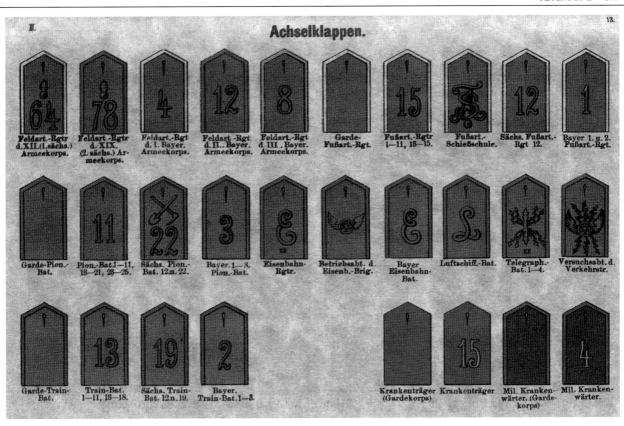

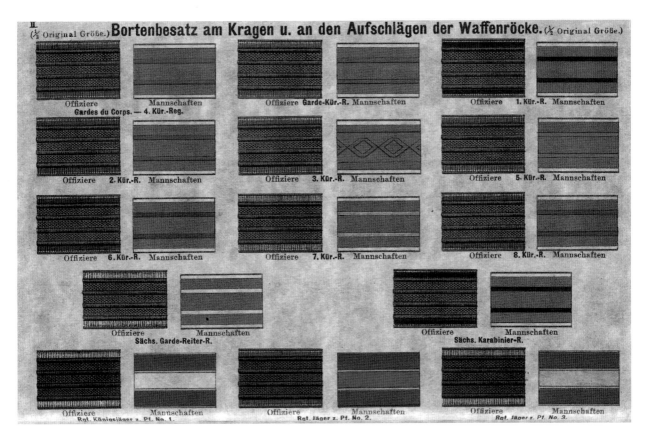

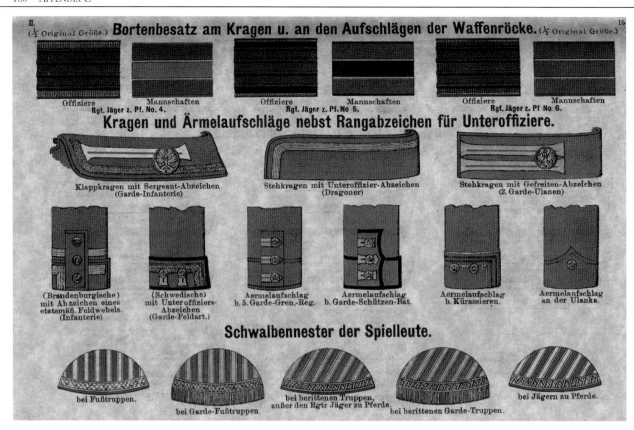

II. (⅓ Original Größe.) **Bortenbesatz am Kragen u. an den Aufschlägen der Waffenröcke.** (⅓ Original Größe.) 15

Offiziere	Mannschaften	Offiziere	Mannschaften	Offiziere	Mannschaften
Rgt. Jäger z. Pf. No. 4.		Rgt. Jäger z. Pf. No 5.		Rgt. Jäger z. Pf No 6.	

Kragen und Ärmelaufschläge nebst Rangabzeichen für Unteroffiziere.

Klappkragen mit Sergeant-Abzeichen (Garde-Infanterie)

Stehkragen mit Unteroffizier-Abzeichen (Dragoner)

Stehkragen mit Gefreiten-Abzeichen (2. Garde-Ulanen)

(Brandenburgische) mit Abzeichen eines etatsmäß. Feldwebels. (Infanterie)

(Schwedische) mit Unteroffiziers-Abzeichen (Garde-Feldart.)

Aermelaufschlag b. 5. Garde-Gren.-Reg.

Aermelaufschlag b. Garde-Schützen-Bat.

Aermelaufschlag b. Kürassieren.

Aermelaufschlag an der Ulanka.

Schwalbennester der Spielleute.

bei Fußtruppen.

bei Garde-Fußtruppen.

bei berittenen Truppen, außer den Rgtr Jäger zu Pferde.

bei berittenen Garde-Truppen.

bei Jägern zu Pferde.

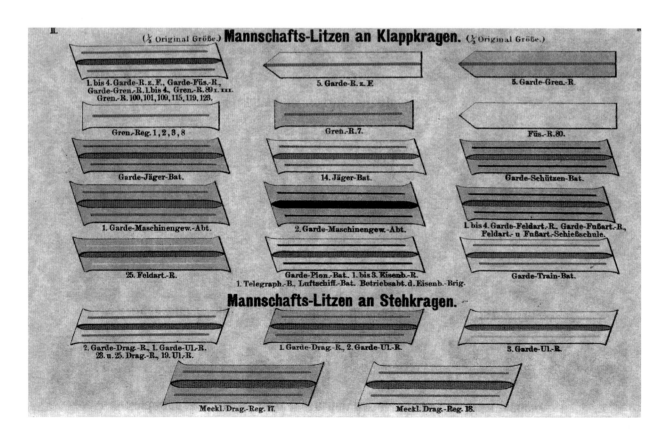

II. (⅓ Original Größe.) **Mannschafts-Litzen an Klappkragen.** (⅓ Original Größe.)

1. bis 4. Garde-R. z. F., Garde-Füs.-R., Garde-Gren.-R. 1 bis 4, Gren.-R. 89 I. u. III. Gren.-R. 100, 101, 109, 115, 119, 123.

5. Garde-R. z. F

5. Garde-Gren.-R.

Gren.-Reg. 1, 2, 3, 8

Gren.-R. 7.

Füs.-R. 80.

Garde-Jäger-Bat.

14. Jäger-Bat.

Garde-Schützen-Bat.

1. Garde-Maschinengew.-Abt.

2. Garde-Maschinengew.-Abt.

1. bis 4. Garde-Feldart.-R., Garde-Fußart.-R., Feldart.- u Fußart.-Schießschule.

25. Feldart.-R.

Garde-Pion.-Bat. 1. bis 3. Eisenb.-R. 1. Telegraph.-B., Luftschiff.-Bat. Betriebsabt. d. Eisenb.-Brig.

Garde-Train-Bat.

Mannschafts-Litzen an Stehkragen.

2. Garde-Drag.-R., 1. Garde-Ul.-R. 23. u. 25. Drag.-R., 19. Ul.-R.

1. Garde-Drag.-R., 2. Garde-Ul.-R.

3. Garde-Ul.-R.

Meckl. Drag.-Reg. 17.

Meckl. Drag.-Reg. 18.

APPENDIX

THE PRUSSIANIZATION
OF THE AMERICAS:
A BRIEF OVERVIEW

With the victory of Germany over France in 1871, many countries began to emulate the uniform styles, tactics and equipment of the Kaiser's armies. The element most frequently and obviously copied was the distinctive *Pickelhaube*. Many countries either copied directly or made variations on the German spiked helmet. Sweden (1845), Norway (1845), Russia (1846), Romanian Moldau (1847), Denmark (1851) and Spain (1855) adopted the spiked helmet prior to the Franco-Prussian War. The many countries which followed suit included the United States of America (1872), England (1878), Portugal (1885), Brazil (1889), Chile (1890), Argentina (1900) and Mexico (1910). To this day, the *Pickelhaube* is still worn in Sweden, Spain and a few Latin American countries.

Latin America was eager to obtain anything German, from military training to uniforms, and eventually became the main client for German arms manufacturers. In 1886 German military advisers, under the leadership of Captain Emil Körner, were asked to organize and train the Chilean Army. The Chileans embraced the Prussianization of their armed forces. Once the Chilean Army had mastered German military drills and even adopted Prussian military customs, it began to spread its new-found identity to other Latin American nations by sending over its own military advisers!

Almost every Latin American country adopted a variation on the Gewehr 1893 and 1898 Bolt Action Rifles manufactured by Mauser and Deutsche Waffen-und-Munition (DWM). Even the United States adopted the M1903 Springfield Rifle that was based on the Mauser. During the Chaco War (1932–5) thirty thousand Bolivian soldiers, trained by German General Hans von Kundt, attacked Paraguay. Even with the aid of Krupp Cannons and Aircraft the Bolivians were driven back by the Paraguayans. The German influence on uniforms of the Bolivian Army was so strong that after the departure of General Kundt military missions from Spain and Czechoslovakia failed to make any impact. However, the Bolivians did influence a German military adviser, Ernst Röhm, in the design of an insignia for the head of Hitler's Brownshirts or Sturmabteilung (SA), consisting of a star-shaped emblem based on the collar tabs worn by Bolivian generals.

With the defeat of imperial Germany in World War I, the influence of the Prussians in Latin America began to wane through the 1920s and 1930s. Interestingly, Argentina and Chile nonetheless adopted the German Model 1935 Steel Helmet when war broke out in 1939. Supplies became harder, and the

South American nations began manufacturing fiber versions of the helmet in order to continue its use for parades. A few Latin American countries quietly supported Germany during World War II, such as Juan Perón's Argentina, only to give tacit support to the Allies when Germany's fortunes began to turn for the worse. Despite Germany's defeat in the two World Wars, the Chilean Armed Forces still display a strong Prussian militaristic influence that is more prevalent than in any other Latin American country.

"On national holidays and important ceremonial occasions the famous old Paradeschritt (The Prussian 'Goose-Step') pounds rhythmically on the paving stones of squares and avenidas. Even the military marches have kept their original Prussian character, though Spanish words have been substituted for German."[‡] Today, cadets of the military academies of Chile, Colombia and Ecuador still wear the *Pickelhaube*, as well as the nineteenth-century Prussian-style uniforms. To this day, many *Pickelhauben*, shakos, parade and field helmets, uniforms, gorgets, insignia and edged weapons used for special occasions are still being made to order by a limited number of craftsmen in Germany for these proud Latin American soldiers who uphold the traditional belief that "Made in Germany" means quality.

Above. While the Germans were a very strong influence in the Americas, they did have some slight influence in the uniforms, equipment and weapons of other armies elsewhere in the world, especially in China. The Chinese had been loyal clients of the German small-arms industry since the turn of the nineteenth century. At the outbreak of World War II the Chinese were armed with German or locally man-ufactured small arms such as the Model 98k Rifle, Maxim Machine Gun and the Model C96 "Broomhandle" Mauser Pistol. These Chinese soldiers are wearing the German Model 1935 Steel Helmets; the Chinese Army also adopted a cap based on the German mountain cap

[‡]D'Ami, *World Uniforms in Colour*

Above. An Argentinian cadet with the *Pickelhaube* adopted in 1900. Note the distinctive Prussian-style epaulettes

Above. Well into the 1930s and through the 1950s the Argentinian Army wore a uniform similar to that worn by the Reichsheer of the 1920s and early 1930s. Of interest is the adoption of the Guard-style double *Kapellenlitzen* on the collar with appropriate *Waffenfarbe* or branch-of-service color

Right. An Argentinian Color Guard wearing the Model 1935 German Helmet. In some cases the standard bearer wore a German-style gorget bearing the Argentinian coat of arms, although it was discontinued in the years following the War. Note the decals bearing Argentinian colors worn on the sides of the helmets

Above. In 1910 Mexico adopted the *Pickelhaube*, continuing to use it until 1920. Seen here is the Color Guard of the 29th Infantry Battalion, armed with Mauser Mexican Model 1910 Rifles, during the rule of Porfirio Díaz at the time of the outbreak of the Mexican Revolution

Above. Some nations were not influenced by German military doctrine, even if they adopted particular uniform styles, equipment and/or weapons. These Finnish soldiers are wearing German Model 1916/18 Steel Helmets. Other armies that adopted German helmets were from young countries born after the Great War, which bought up the abundant German war surplus at bargain prices. Among the countries using these helmets were the Baltic states, Hungary and Ireland. Interestingly, the Irish Army wore these helmets with British-style uniforms and equipment, and when supplies were growing scarcer, new versions were remanufactured in England!

Above. The uniform and cap worn by this senior Mexican officer shows strong German influences

Above. Even in 1939 the Chilean Army still maintained a strong Prussian influence in its bearing as well as its uniforms. Note the strongly German-influenced shoulder-boards worn by this Chilean officer. The Chilean Army has retained much of its German influence well into the twenty-first century

Above. General Juan Vicente Gómez, Venezuela's constitutional president from 1908 to 1935. This photograph, taken prior to the advent of World War I, shows his uniform and insignia, and in particular his strongly Prussian-influenced sword, which had been left to him by German and Chilean military missions that helped to form the Venezuelan Army into an efficient force from 1892 to 1910. The sword is typical of the infantry officer's models made available for export by Solingen edged weapons manufacturers like WKC, Carl Kaiser, E. & F. Hörster and Carl Eickhorn

Above. This Californian militiaman from San Francisco is wearing imported German *Pickelhaube*, *c.*1880. Note the distinctive Prussian-style American Eagle helmet plate. The US Model 1872 Uniform is of the style adopted by the United States Army and state militias in the mid-1870s, and display a strong German influence in such elements as the Brandenburg-style cuffs on the tunic, branch-of-service colors (*Waffenfarbe*) on the cuffs and collar, and the epaulettes. The edged weapon is a Model 1860 Line and Staff Officers' Sword. The star-shaped medal identifies him as a Civil War veteran and a member of the Grand Army of the Republic (GAR). The *Pickelhaube* appears to be of the 1867 style with the rounded front visor. Interestingly, various models from 1842 to 1887 are known to have been used by American militia units between the Civil and Spanish-American Wars. (*Courtesy Mark Kasal*)

ACKNOWLEDGEMENTS

I would like to thank the following individuals who have assisted me through the years and have made this work possible: Ron G. Hickox (†); Don Miller (†); Hilary Powell; Malcolm Gordon; Thomas Brackmann; Thomas Faust; Jörn Fickart; Katrina Lattke; Ronny Van Troostenberghe; R. James Bender; Michal Jaroszynski-Wolfram; Richard Bass, Jr; Elke Diederich and Georg Breuer; Bundesministerium der Verteidigung (German Federal Ministry of Defense); Chris Cameron; John Angolia; Lieutenant Colonel Thomas Johnson, USA (Retired); William and Lois Egan; Bolko Hartmann; Robert Tredwen; Alan Smith; David Sullivan; Lionel Leventhal; Michael Leventhal; René Chartrand; Christopher F. Seidler; Malcolm Fisher; Phillip Bühler; Ron Manion; Rick Keller and staff from Great War Militaria; Mark Kasal (Ensign); Anthony Bomba, USN; Edward C. Ezell (†); Martin Windrow; Phillip Jowett; Richard Heller; SS-Sturmbannführer Walter Reder, W-SS (†); Gefreiter Hans Goebler, Kriegesmarine/U-505 (†); Dipl. Ing. Dr Ferdinand Kirchner; Mark Salussolia; A. M. de Quesada, MD; and, to my daughter Caroline.

The following societies and its members from around the world have been gracious in providing guidance during the years researching this work: Traditionsverband ehemaliger Schutz- und überseetruppen/Freunde der früheren deutschen Schutzgebiete e.V. (FRG); Company of Military Historians (USA); Society for Army Historical Research (UK); South Africa Military Historical Society (South Africa); 8th Air Force Historical Society (USA); US Naval Institute; Garand Collector's Association (USA); Historic Naval Ships Association (USA); National Rifle Association (USA); The Sunshine Postcard Collector's Club (USA); Orders and Medals Society of America (USA); American Society of Military Insignia Collectors (USA); The Orders and Medals Research Society (UK).

I would like to gratefully acknowledge the following institutions: Bundeswehr Museum (Dresden, Germany); Bayerisches Armeemuseum Ingolstadt (Ingolstadt, Germany); Das Heeresgeschichtliche Museum (Vienna, Austria); Rainer-Regimentsmuseum, Festung Hohensalzburg (Salzburg, Austria); Deutsches Historisches Museum (Berlin, Germany); Deutsches Klingenmuseum Solingen (Solingen, Germany); Reichsstadt-Museum (Rothenburg o.d.T., Germany); Bayerisches National Museum (Munich, Germany); Deutsches Museum (Munich, Germany); Museum Berlin Karlshorst (Berlin, Germany); Ministry of Defense (Berlin, Germany); National Archives (Washington DC, USA); Library of Congress (Washington DC, USA); National Infantry Museum (Fort Benning, USA); West Point Military Academy Museum (USA); Imperial War Museum (London, UK); National Army Museum (London, UK); Bastogne Historical Center (Bastogne, Belgium); D-Day National Museum (New Orleans, USA); Musée de l'Armée (Paris, France); Musée du Costume Militaire (Thiaucort, France); Musée de la Bataille du Saillant de Saint-Mihiel, 1914–1918 (Thiaucourt, France). These institutions and their staff have been a treasure trove of information, and much of the material they have provided has been incorporated into this work.

Abbott, Peter. *Armies in East Africa, 1914–1918*. London: Osprey, 2002.

Ager, VerKuilen. *Friekorps Insignia*. Rochester, NY: privately published, 1979.

Ailsby, Christopher. *Hitler's Sky Warriors*. Dulles, VA: Brassey's, Inc., 2000.

Altmannsperger, Peter. *Die Soldaten unter dem Edelweiß: Die 1. Gebirgsdivision und die Bundeswehr in Bayern, Eine Bilddokumentation*. Wolfsheim, Germany: RMS-Verlag, 1998.

D'Ami, Rinaldo D. (ed.). *World Uniforms in Colour, Volume Two: Nations of America, Africa, Asia and Oceana*. London: Patrick Stephens Ltd, 1969: 43

Angolia, John, and Schlicht, Adolf. *Die Kriegsmarine, Uniforms & Traditions*, Vols 1–3. San Jose, CA: R. James Bender Publishing, 1991–3.

Bender, Roger James. *Legion Condor: Uniforms, Organization and History*. San Jose, CA: R. James Bender Publishing, 1992.

Bleckwenn, Hans. *Unter dem Preußen-Adler: Das brandenburgisch-preußische Heer, 1640–1807*. München: C. Bertelsmann Verlag GmbH, 1978.

Das Buch der Deutschen Kolonien. Leipzig: Wilhelm Goldman Verlag, 1937.

Buchner, Alex. *The German Infantry Handbook, 1939–1945*. West Chester, PA: Schiffer, 1991.

Buchner, Alex. *Weapons and Equipment of the German Fallschirmtruppe*. Atglen, PA: Schiffer, 1996.

Bueno Carrera, José María. *La División y la Escuadrilla Azul: Su Organización y sus Uniformes*. Madrid, Spain: Aldaba Ediciones, S.A., 1991.

Bueno Carrera, José María. *Uniformes Militares de la Guerra Civil Española*. Madrid: Almena Ediciones, 1997.

Bull, Stephen. *Stormtrooper*. London: Military Illustrated, 1999.

Bull, Stephen. *World War One German Army*. London: Brassy's, 2000.

Bundeswehr Heute: *Uniformen*. Bonn: Das Bundesministerium der Verteidigung, 1993.

Caballero Jurado, Carlos. *Foreign Volunteers of the Wehrmacht, 1941–1945*. London: Osprey, 1983.

Caballero Jurado, Carlos. *The German Freikorps, 1918–1923*. Oxford: Osprey, 2001.

Caballero Jurado, Carlos. "Los Uniformes de la División Azul". Marton, P. and G. Vedelago. *Los Uniformes Alemanes de la Segunda Guerra Mundial*. Barcelona, Spain: Editorial de Vecchi, S.A., 1981.

Cooper, Matthew. *The German Army, 1933–1945*. Lanham, MD: Scarborough House, 1978.

Costley, Bill. *Obergefrieter: Jäger Battalion Light Infantry Division*. San Diego, CA: Last 100 Days E.T.O., 1993.

Davis, Brian Leigh. *Badges & Insignia of the Third Reich, 1933–1945*. Poole: Blandford Press, 1983.

Davis, Brian Leigh. *German Army Uniforms and Insignia, 1933–1945*. London: Arms and Armour Press, 1992. (Second revised edition of 1971 with amendments and corrections.)

Davis, Brian Leigh. *German Combat Uniforms of World War Two*, Vols 1–2. London: Arms and Armour Press, 1984–5.

Davis, Brian Leigh. *German Uniforms of the Third Reich, 1933–1945*. New York: ARCO Publishing, Inc., 1980.

Davis, Brian Leigh. *NATO Forces: An Illustrated Reference to Their Organization and Insignia*. London: Blandford Press, 1988.

de Quesada, Alejandro Manuel. "The Austrian U-Boat Service, 1907–1918". *Military Trader*, Vol. 5, Issue 3 (March 1998): 46–8.

de Quesada, Alejandro Manuel. "The Austrian U-Boat Service, Badge: 1910–1918". *The Military Advisor*, Vol. 7, No. 1 (Winter 1995–6): 33–5.

de Quesada, Alejandro Manuel. "Deutsche Feuerwehr Belt Buckles, 1900–1989". *Military Trader*, Vol. 7, Issue 10 (October 2000): 32–3.

de Quesada, Alejandro Manuel. *Eickhorn Export Edged Weapons, Volume One: Latin America*. Union City, TN: Pioneer Press, 1996.

de Quesada, Alejandro Manuel. "Fuerwehr Pickelhaubes of Pre-Nazi Germany". *Bits 'n' Pieces*, Vol. 1, Issue 4 (March 1993): 3, 11.

de Quesada, Alejandro Manuel. "Soldiers of the Reich in Tampa Bay". *Pastimes*, Vol. 2, No. 1 (Fall 1995): 9.

de Quesada, Alejandro Manuel. *Uniforms of the German Soldier: An Illustrated History from World War II to the Present Day*. London: Greenhill Books, 2006.

de Smet, J. L. *Uniformen des Heeres, 1933–1945*. Kedichem: Military Collectors' Service, 1972.

Die Deutsche Armee vor dem Weltkriege. Leipzig: Verlag von Moritz Ruhl, 1926.

Deutsche Kämpfen in Spanien: Herausgegeben von der Legion Condor. Berlin: Wilhelm Limpert-Verlag, 1939.

Die Deutsche Reichswehr. Leipzig: Verlag von Moritz Ruhl, 1919.

Die Deutsche Reichswehr. Leipzig: Verlag von Moritz Ruhl, 1921.

Deutsche Uniformabzeichen, 1900–1945. Norderstedt: Militair-Verlag Klaus D. Patzwall, 1994.

Deutsche Uniformen: Heer, Marine, Luftwaffe, Arbeitsdienst, SS, SA, NSFK, NSKK, RLB, HJ, DJ, Polizei und Gendarmerie. Leipzig: Verlag von Moritz Ruhl, 1938.

Deutsches Soldatenjahrbuch 1965. München-Lochhausen: Schild-Verlag, 1964.

Doehle, Dr Heinrich. *Die Auszeichnungen des Großdeutschen Reichs: Orden, Ehrenzeichen, Abzeichen*. Berlin: E. O. Erdmenger & Co. K.G., 1943.

Doehle, Dr Heinrich (translator: Hamelman, William E.). *Medals & Decorations of the Third Reich: Orders, Decorations, Badges*. Denison, TX: Reddick Enterprises, 1995. (Reprint of the German 1943 edition.)

Edward, Roger. *German Airborne Troops*. Garden City, NY: Doubleday & Co., 1974.

Die Ehemaligen Kaiserlich Deutschen Schutztruppen. Leipzig: Verlag von Moritz Ruhl, 1910.

Eisenhart Rothe, Alexander von. *Ehrendenkmal der Deutschen Armee und Marine*. Berlin: Deutscher National-Verlag, 1931.

Ellis, Chris. *21st Panzer Division: Rommel's Afrika Korps Spearhead*. Hersham: Ian Allen, 2001.

Feist, Uwe, and Harms, Norman. *Fallschirmjäger in Action*. Carrollton, TX: Squadron/Signal Publications, Inc., 1973.

Figueroa, J. R. *Tropical Headgear of the Wehrmacht in W.W. II*. Los Angeles, CA: Figueroa Creations, 1996.

Figueroa, J. R. *Tropical Uniforms of the German Army and Airforce in W.W. II*. Los Angeles, CA: Figueroa Creations, 1993.

Fosten, D. S. V. *Cuirassiers and Heavy Cavalry: Dress Uniforms of the German Imperial Cavalry, 1900–1914*. London: Almark Publishing Co., 1972.

The German Forces in the Field, November 1918. London: Imperial War Museum, 1995. (Originally published in 1918, 7th revision, by the War Office.)

Graudenz, Karlheinz, and Schindler, Hanns-Michael. *Die Deutschen Kolonien*. Augsburg: Weltbild Verlag GmbH, 1988.

Die Graue Felduniform der Deutschen Armee. Leipzig: Verlag von Moritz Ruhl, 1910.

Hagger, D. H. *Hussars and Mounted Rifles: Uniforms of the Imperial German Cavalry, 1900–1914*. London: Almark Publishing Co., 1974.

Handbook of German Uniforms: The German Army and Luftwaffe. Harrisburg, PA: A.A.F.I.S., 1942.

Handbook of the German Army (Home and Colonial). London: Imperial War Museum, 2002. (Originally published in 1914 by the War Office.)

Handbuch Militärisches Grundwissen, NVA-Ausgabe. Berlin: Militärverlag der Deutschen Demokratischen Republik, 1988.

Harms, Norman. *German Infantry in Action*. Carrollton, TX: Squadron/Signal Publications, Inc., 1973.

Haß, Dietrich, and Hocke, Michael. *Die Prussische Polizei*. Flensburg: privately published, 1986.

Haupt, Werner. *Die Deutsche Schutztruppe 1889–1918*. Gerg am See: Türmer Verlag, 1989.

Hicks, Major James E. *German Weapons-Uniforms-Insignia 1841–1918*. La Canada, CA: James E. Hicks & Son, 1964.

Hicks, Major James E. *Notes on German Ordnance, 1841–1918*. La Canada, CA: James E. Hicks & Son, 1937.

Hoffschmidt, E. J., and Tantum, W. H., *German Army and Navy Uniforms & Insignia, 1871–1918*. Old Greenwich, CT: WE, Inc., 1968.

Hormann, Jörg M. *German Uniforms of the 20th Century, Vol. 1: Uniforms of the Panzer Troops, 1917 to the Present*. West Chester, PA: Schiffer, 1989.

Hormann, Jörg M. *German Uniforms of the 20th Century, Vol. 2: Uniforms of the Panzer Troops, 1917 to the Present*. West Chester, PA: Schiffer, 1989.

Hormann, Jörg M. *Uniformen der Infanterie, 1919 bis Heute*. Friedberg: Podzun-Pallas-Verlag GmbH, 1989.

Hormann, Jörg M. *Uniformen der Panzertruppe, 1917 bis Heute*. Friedberg: Podzun-Pallas-Verlag GmbH, 1989.

Jahrbuch des Deutschen Heeres 1939. Leipzig: Verlag von Breitkopf & Härtel, 1938.

Jurado, Carlos Caballero. *The German Freikorps, 1918–1923*. Oxford: Osprey, 2001.

Kaltenegger, Roland. *Weapons and Equipment of the German Mountain Troops*. Atglen, PA: Schiffer, 1995.

Keubke, Klaus-Ulrich. *Uniformen der Nationalen Volksarmee der DDR, 1956–1986*. Berlin: Brandenburgisches Verlagshaus, 1990.

Kinna, H., and Moss, D. A. *Jäger & Schützen: Dress and Distinctions, 1910–1914*. Watford: Bellona Publications (Argus Books), 1977.

Das Kleine Buch vom Deutschen Heere. Leipzig: Verlag von Lipsius & Tischer, 1901.

Knötel, Richard, Knötel, Herbert, and Sieg, Herbert. *Farbiges Handbuch der Uniformkunde*. Stuttgart: W. Spemann, 1985.

Knötel, Richard, Knötel, Herbert, and Sieg, Herbert. *Uniforms of the World*. New York: Charles Scribners's Sons, 1980.

Kolonialkriegerdank-Kalander für das Jahr 1917. Berlin: Verlag des Kolonialkriegerdank E.B., 1917.

Kopenhagen, Wilfried. *Die Landstreitkräfte der NVA*. Stuttgart: Motorbuch Verlag, 1999.

Large, David Clay. *Germans to the Front: West German Rearmament in the Adenauer Era*. Chapel Hill, NC: The University of North Carolina Press, 1996.

Layton, Geoff. *From Bismarck to Hitler: Germany 1890–1933*. London: Hodder & Stoughton, 2002.

Layton, Geoff. *Germany: The Third Reich 1933–45*. London: Hodder & Stoughton, 2000.

Long, Richard C. "Leibhussaren (LH) to Leibstandarte (LAH)". *The Military Advisor*, Vol. 14, No. 4 (fall 2003): 4–13.

Lorch, Carlos. *Im bunten Rock: Militärisches Zeremoniell in 16 Nationen*. Stuttgart: Motorbuch Verlag, 1997.

Marcks, Otto. *Die Bundeswehr im Aufbau*. Bonn, Germany: Athenäum-Verlag, 1957.

Marrion, R. J. *Lancers and Dragoons: Uniforms of the Imperial German Cavalry, 1900–1914*. London: Almark Publishing Co., 1975.

Marton, P., and Vedelago, G., *Los Uniformes Alemanes de la Segunda Guerra Mundial*. Barcelona: Editorial de Vecchi, S.A., 1981.

Meybauer, Paul. *Die Helmwappen und Namenszüge der Deutschen Armee*. Leipzig: Verlag von Moritz Ruhl, 1910.

Nachtrage und Berichtigungen zum Deutschen Reichsheer. Berlin: Max Hochsprung, 1892.

Nash, David. *German Artillery, 1914–1918*. London: Almark Publishing Co., 1970.

Die Nebeltruppe: Waffenhefte des Heeres, Herausgegeben vom Oberkommando des Heeres. München: Deutscher Volksverlag GMBH, 1939.

Die Neue Deutsche Reichswehr, Die Freiwilligen-Verbände und ihre Charakteristischen Abzeichen. Leipzig: Verlag von Moritz Ruhl, 1919.

Neumann, Thomas F. "Modern German Army SSI Background." *The Trading Post*, Vol. 72, No. 4 (October–December 2003): 45–8.

Oberkommando des Heeres. *Liste der Fertigungskennzeichen für Waffen, Munition und Gerät*. Berlin: Gedruckt im Oberkommando des Heeres, 1944.

Oliver, Tony L. *D.D.R. Collectors' Reference Guides, 1949–1990*, Vol. 1. Eton Wick: T.L.O. Publications, 1993.

Ortenburg, Georg. *Mit Gott für König und Vaterland: Das preußische Heer, 1807–1914*. München: C. Bertelsmann Verlag GmbH, 1979.

Palinckx, Werner. *Camouflage Uniforms of the German Wehrmacht*. Atglen, PA: Schiffer, 2002.

Pawlas, Karl R. (ed.). *Liste der Fertigungskennzeichen für Waffen, Munition und Gerät*. Nürnberg: Publizistisches Archiv für Militär- und Waffenwesen, 1977.

Pawley, Ronald. *The Kaiser's Warlords: German Commanders of World War I*. Oxford: Osprey, 2003.

Peter, Nash. *German Belt Buckles, 1845–1945: Buckles of the Enlisted Ranks*. Atglen, PA: Schiffer, 2003.

Peterson, Daniel. *Waffen SS Camouflage Uniforms & Post-War Derivatives*. London: Windrow & Greene, 1995.

Peterson, Daniel. *Wehrmacht Camouflage Uniforms & Post-War Derivatives*. London: Windrow & Greene, 1995.

Petschull, Jürgen. *Der Wahn vom Weltreich: Die Geschichte der deutschen Kolonien*. Hamburg: STERN-Buch im Verlag Gruner Jahr AG & Co., 1984.

Quarrie, Bruce. *German Airborne Troops, 1939–1945*. London: Osprey, 1983.

Queen, Eric. *Red Shines the Sun: A Pictorial History of the Fallschirm-Infanterie*. San Jose, CA: R. James Bender Publishing, 2002.

Radecke, Erich. *Geschichte des Polizei-Tschakos: Von der Alten Armee zur Polizei*. Hamburg: Selbstverlag des Autors, 1995.

Ramos, Raúl Arias. *La Legión Cóndor: Imágenes inéditas para su historia*. Madrid: Agualarga Editores, S.L., 2002.

Reddick, J. Rex. (ed.) *F. W. Assman & Söhne Sales Catalog*. Denison, TX: Reddick Enterprises, 1992. (Reprint of 1930s Catalog.)

Redmon, Ronald L., and Cuccarese, James F. *Panzergrenadiers in Action*. Carrollton, TX: Squadron/Signal Publications, Inc., 1980.

Reibert, Dr jur. W., Hauptmann (Heer). *Der Dienst-Unterricht im Heere: Ausgabe für den Gewehr- und L.M.G.–Schützen*. Berlin: E. S. Mittler & Sohn, 1937.

Reibert, Dr jur. W., Major (Heer). *Der Dienst-Unterricht im Heere: Ausgabe für den Nachrichtensoldaten*. Berlin: E. S. Mittler & Sohn, 1938.

Reibert, Dr jur. W., Major (Heer). *Der Dienst-Unterricht im Heere: Ausgabe für den Schützen der Schützenkompanie*. Berlin: E. S. Mittler & Sohn, 1938.

Reibert, Dr jur. W., Major (Heer). *Der Dienst-Unterricht im Heere: Ausgabe für den Schützen der Schützenkompanie*. Berlin: E. S. Mittler & Sohn, 1940.

Reibert, Dr jur. W., Hauptmann (Heer). *Der Dienst-Unterricht im Heere: Ausgabe für den S.M.G.–Schützen*. Berlin: E. S. Mittler & Sohn, 1937.

Der Reibert: Das Handbuch für den Deutschen Soldaten. Hamburg: E. S. Mittler & Sohn, 1999.

Der Reibert: Das Handbuch für den Soldaten (Ausgabe Marine). Herford: E. S. Mittler & Sohn, 1979.

Der Reichsorganisationsleiter der NSDAP. *Organisationsbuch der NSDAP.* München: Zentralverlag der NSDAP, 1943.

Ripley, Tim. *The Wehrmacht: The German Army of World War II, 1939–1945.* New York: Fitzroy Dearborn, 2003.

Rosignoli, Guido. *Army Badges and Insignia of World War Two.* New York: Macmillan, 1972.

Rosignoli, Guido. *Army Badges and Insignia since 1945.* New York: Macmillan, 1973.

Rottman, Gordon L. *Warsaw Pact Ground Forces.* London: Osprey, 1987.

Rottman, Gordon L. *World Special Forces Insignia.* London: Osprey, 1989.

Schulze, Carl. *IFOR: Allied Forces in Bosnia.* London: Windrow & Greene, 1996.

Seaton, Albert. *The Army of the German Empire, 1870–1888.* London: Osprey, 1973.

Sigel, Gustav A. (Dr. J. J. Breuilly, ed.). *German Military Forces of the 19th Century: The Armament, Insignia and Uniforms of the Army and Navy Illustrated in Full Color.* New York: The Military Press, 1989.

Sigel, Gustav A. *Germany's Army and Navy by Pen and Picture.* Chicago: The Werner Company, 1900.

Simpson, Keith. *History of the German Army.* London: Bison Books, 1985.

Smith, Digby. *NATO Uniforms Today.* London: Arms and Armour Press, 1984.

Soukup, Walter and Th. Thomas. *Uniformen und militärische Symbole des 20. Jahrhunderts.* Rastatt: Erich Pabel Verlag GmbH, 1982.

Stephens, F. J., and Maddocks, Graham J. *Uniforms and Organisation of the Imperial German Army, 1900–1918.* London: Almark Publishing Co., 1975.

Steven, Andrew, and Amodio, Peter. *Waffen-SS in Colour Photographs.* London: Windrow & Greene, 1990.

Stiles, Andrina, and Farmer, Alan. *The Unification of Germany, 1815–90.* London: Hodder & Stoughton, 2001.

Thomas, Nigel. *The German Army 1939–1945 (1): Bliztkrieg.* London: Osprey, 1998.

Thomas, Nigel. *The German Army 1939–1945 (2): North Africa & Balkans.* London: Osprey, 1998.

Thomas, Nigel. *The German Army 1939–1945 (3): Eastern Front 1941–1943.* London: Osprey, 1999.

Thomas, Nigel. *The German Army 1939–1945 (4): Eastern Front 1943–1945.* London: Osprey, 1999.

Thomas, Nigel. *The German Army 1939–1945 (5): Western Front 1943–1945.* London: Osprey, 2000.

Thomas, Nigel. *The German Army in World War I: (1) 1914–1915.* Oxford: Osprey, 2003.

Thomas, Nigel. *The German Army in World War I: (2) 1915–1917.* Oxford: Osprey, 2004.

Thomas, Nigel. *NATO Armies Today.* London: Osprey, 1987.

Thompson, Leroy. *Badge & Insignia of the Elite Forces.* London: Arms and Armour Press, 1991.

Tophoven, Rolf. *GSG 9: German Response to Terrorism.* Koblenz: Bernard & Graefe Verlag, 1984.

Uniformen und Abzeichen der Deutschen Bundeswehr, 1956. (No information on which agency published this pamphlet.)

Die Uniformen und Abzeichen der SA, SS und des Stahlhelm, Brigade Ehrhardt, Hitler-Jugend, Amtswalter, Abgeordnete, NSBO und NSKK. Berlin: Traditions-Verlag Kolf & Co., 1937.

Unsere NVA, Ausgabe 1989. Berlin: Militärverlag der DDR, 1988.

Vogenbeck, Peter, and Eugen, Pauls. *Die Adlerstempel von Deutsch-Südwestafrika.* Kalenborn-Scheuern/Münster: privately published, 1995.

Walter, John. *Military Rifles of Two World Wars.* London: Greenhill Books, 2003.

Walther, Klaus. *Uniformeffekten der bewaffneten Organe der DDR, Band I: Ministerium des Innern, 1949–1990.* Berlin: ECOTOUR Verlag GmbH, 1993.

Walther, Klaus. *Uniformeffekten der bewaffneten Organe der DDR, Band II: Ministerium für Nationale Verteidigung, 1956–1990/ Ministerium für Staatssicherheit, 1957–1989.* Berlin: ECOTOUR Verlag GmbH, 1994.

Wilkins, Gary. *The Collector's Guide to Cloth Third Reich Military Headgear.* Atglen, PA: Schiffer, 2002.

Williamson, Gordon. *German Army Elite Units, 1939–1945.* London: Osprey, 2002.

Woolley, Charles. *German Uniforms, Insignia & Equipment, 1918–1923: Freikorps, Reichsheer, Vehicles, Weapons.* Atglen, PA: Schiffer, 2002.

Woolley, Charles. *The Kaiser's Army in Color: Uniforms of the Imperial German Army as Illustrated by Carl Becker, 1890–1910.* Atglen, PA: Schiffer, 2000.

Woolley, Charles. *Uniforms & Equipment of the Imperial German Army as Illustrated by Carl Becker, 1900–1918.* Atglen, PA: Schiffer, 1999.

Zaloga, Steven J., and Loop, James. *Soviet Bloc Elite Forces.* London: Osprey, 1985.

Zilian, Frederick. *From Confrontation to Cooperation: The Takeover of the National People's (East German) Army by the Bundeswehr.* Westport, CT: Praeger, 1999.

GLOSSARY

Abteilung. Detachment, department, or battalion.

Abzeichen. Badge

Allerhöchste Kabinetts-Ordre (AKO). Highest Cabinet Order or Directive.

Armee. Army.

Armee-Abteilung. Army Detachment.

Armeegruppe. Army Group.

Artillerie. Artillery.

Arzt. Doctor.

Aufklärung. Reconnaissance.

Bandeau. Ribbon.

Bataillon. Battalion.

Batterie. Battery.

Baupionier. Construction Engineer.

Befehlshaber der. Commander of . . .

Beil. Hatchets.

Beilpike. Pick hatchets.

Brigade. Brigade.

Brotbeutel. Bread bag or haversack.

Chef des Generalstabes. Chief of the General Staff.

Division. Division.

Dolch. Dagger.

Einheit. Detachment or unit.

Eisenbahn. Railroad.

Ersatz. Replacement or substitute.

Fahne. Flag, standard.

Fahnenträger. Standard Bearer.

Fahrtruppen. Fast Troops.

Fallschirm. Parachute.

Fallschirmjäger. Paratrooper.

Fangschnur. Cords of aiguillette.

Feld. Field.

Feldflasche. Canteen.

Feldgendarmerie. Field Police.

Feldgrau. Field-grey.

Feldjäger. Infantryman.

Feldkommandantur. Field Command.

Feldlazarett. Field Hospital.

Feldmarshall. Field Marshal.

Feldmütze. Field cap.

Feldpost. Field post.

Feldwebel. Sergeant.

Filzhaube. Felt helmet.

Flak. From *Fliegerabwehrkanone*, meaning anti-aircraft gun.

Flieger. Flyer, pilot.

Fliegerstutzhelm. Reinforced flight helmet.

Flügelmütze. Winged hat.

Freiwillige. Volunteer.

Führer. Leader.

Fusilier. Infantry or Heavy Infantry. A traditional term for a type of infantryman.

Garde. Guard.

Gebirg. Mountain.

Gebirgsjäger. Mountain Trooper.

Gefreiter. Corporal.

Geheime. Secret.

General. General.

Generalkommando. General Headquarters.

Generalstab des Heeres. Army General Staff.

Gepäck. Luggage.

Geschütz. Gun.

Gesellschaft. Society, organization, company.

Gewehr. Gun, rifle.

Granatwerfer. Mortar.

Grenadier. A traditional term for a type of infantryman.

Grenztruppen. Border Guard Troops.

Gruppe. Group.

Halsbinde. A cravat of black lasting which buckles behind the neck.

Hauptmann. Captain.

Heer. Army.

Heeresgruppe. Army Group.

Helmwappen. Helmet plate.

Hut. Hat.

Jäger. Literal meaning "hunter" but usually applied to Light Infantry.

Jäger zu Pferde. Mounted Dispatch Rider.

Kaiserwehr. Armed Forces of Imperial Germany, 1871–1918.

Kampf. Struggle.

Kavallerie. Cavalry.

Kettenkrad. Tracked motorcycle.

Knebel. Toggle.

Kochgeschirr. Individual camp kettle or mess-kit.

Kokarde. Cockade.

Koller. A short boiled-wool jacket worn by members of the German heavy, Kürassier regiments.

Kolpak. Busby bag.

Kommandeur. A person commanding a unit.

Kommando. Headquarters or command.

Kompanie. Company.

Koppelschloß. Belt buckle.

Kugelhelm. Ball helmet, generic name for Artillery *Pickelhaube*.

Kürassier. Heavy Cavalry.

Krieg. War

Kriegesgefangene. Prisoner of war.

Kriegsmarine. Navy during the Third Reich.

Landeskokarde. State cockade.

Landsturm. Home Guard Troops.

Landswehr. Territorial Reserve.

Lebensmittelbeutel. Ration pocket in a knapsack.

Leibriemen. Leather belt.

Leutnant. Lieutenant.

Lieb. Life.

Liebstandarte. Bodyguard Regiment.

Litewka. Jacket.

Litzen. Braid or piping.

Luftwaffe. Air Force.

Major. Major.

Offizier. Officer.

Orden. Decoration, orders (medals).

Patronenbehälter. Pockets for cartridges in a knapsack.

Patrontasche. Cartridge box.

Pelzmütze. Fur hat.

Perlring. Pearl ring.

Pickelhaube. Spiked helmet.

Portepee. Dagger or sword knot.

Rabatte. Covering.

Raupenhelm. Caterpillar helmet.

Regiment. Regiment.

Reichskokarde. National cockade.

Ringkragen. Gorget.

äbel. Saber.

Schirmmütze. Visor cap.

Schnuren. Cord or string.

Schnürschuhe. A pair of easy shoes of supple tan leather.

Schutzen. Sharpshooters.

Schutztruppe. Literally "Protection Troops", usually applied to colonial troops.

Schwalbennester. Swallows' nests.

Seebataillon. Sea Battalion, Imperial German Naval Infantry.

Soldat. Soldier, Private.

Sonderführer. Warrant Officer.

Spaten. Spade.

Stahlhelm. Helmet.

Standart. Standard, regimental flag.

Stiefel. A pair of boots.

Tarbusch. A zinc-and-copper alloy.

Technik. Technology, engineering.

Tornister. Knapsack.

Tornisterbeutel. Ration bag.

Trichter. Plume holder.

Trinkbecher. Drinking cup.

Troddel. Bayonet knot.

Tropenhelm. Pith helmet.

Tschako. Shako.

Tschapka. German term for the Uhlan Helmet (*czapka*).

Tuchhose. Trousers.

Unterfeldwebel. Sergeant, Non-Commissioned Officer.

Unterseeboot. Submarine.

Volk. People.

Wäschebeutel. Compartment for clothes.

Waffen. Weapon, arms.

Waffenfarbe. Branch of Service Color.

Waffenrock. Tunic.

Wappen. Device. The *Wappen* is the state device found on the front of a *Pickelhaube*.

Werft. Dockyard.

Zelt-ausrustüng. Individual tent.

Zeltbahn. Shelter-tent.

Zeltstock. Tent poles.

Zeltzubehörbeutel. Shelter-tent accessories case in a knapsack.

Zoll. Customs.